Signs and Wonders

Signs and Wonders

Religious Rhetoric and the Preservation of Sign Language

Tracy Ann Morse

Gallaudet University Press
Washington, DC

Gallaudet University Press
Washington, DC 20002
http://gupress.gallaudet.edu

Printed in the United States of America

Library of Congress Cataloging-in-Publication Data

Morse, Tracy Ann.
Signs and wonders : religious rhetoric and the preservation of sign language / Tracy Ann Morse.
pages cm
Includes bibliographical references and index.
ISBN 978-1-56368-601-6 (pbk. : alk. paper) — ISBN 978-1-56368-602-3 (e-book)
1. American Sign Language—Religious aspects. 2. Church work with the deaf—United States. 3. Deaf—United States—Religious life. I. Title.
HV2476.4.M67 2014
419′.7—dc23
2013042676

Cover photographs from "The Lord's Prayer in the Sign Language," *The Silent Worker*, April 1912, 125. Courtesy of Gallaudet University Archives.

♾ The paper used in this publication meets the minimum requirements of American National Standard for Information Sciences—Permanence of Paper for Printed Library Materials, ANSI Z39.48-1984.

Dedicated to the memory of
my dad, Gary Allan Morse, Sr.

Contents

Preface

THIS book examines religious arguments for the preservation and use of sign language in historical documents and contemporary experiences related to deaf education, church ministries and congregations for deaf people, and activism in the deaf community. In all of these venues, religious rhetoric empowers the deaf community to advocate for the use and recognition of sign language. Historically, the deaf community in the United States has been oppressed by a dominant hearing community that has sought to control deaf Americans' use of language. The influence of religion has helped the deaf community to acquire a language that encourages others to support the use and recognition of sign language.

Although this project has a specific focus at the intersections of deafness, religion, and rhetoric, it is important to acknowledge the scholarship that leads to these intersections and influences my selection of the locations I examine—schools, the sanctuary, and the social activism of deaf people. Specifically, I owe a debt of gratitude to the important work that has been carried out in deaf studies and rhetorical studies.

I am also grateful to those who have supported me in making this book. This project started with a research grant from the University of Arizona when I was a graduate student. That grant allowed me to do archival research at Gallaudet University, which resulted in a dissertation and then this book using the evidence I found. I am indebted to the librarians and archivist at the Gallaudet University Library, especially in the Deaf Collections and Archives. I have been able to complete this project with research support from my current institution, East Carolina University.

There have also been many friends who have listened, read, and advised throughout this process of researching and writing. I am thankful for my mentors Roxanne Mountford and Brenda Jo Brueggemann who both pushed me when this book was just an idea to research. Patty Malesh, Claire Lauer, Gwen Gray Schwartz, Bo Wang, and Michelle F. Eble helped me at various stages of thinking, drafting, and revising for which I am grateful. For my cheerleaders, my family, this project is as much yours as it is mine. For their encouragement, I thank my parents, Gary and Betty Morse and brother, Allan Morse. Above all, I thank Billy Humphreys for his unending love and pep talks

Signs and Wonders

Introduction

WHEN I was a child growing up in the 1970s, my family had a Sunday morning routine. My brother and I would watch Popeye cartoons until we had to get ready for church. While we were cleaning up and changing, my mother or father would change the TV channel to a televised church service. When I was dressed and ready, I would go back and sit in front of the TV until it was time to leave. I didn't watch the preacher standing behind the pulpit, but I did watch the sign language interpreter sharing the screen. My first exposure to the deaf community in the United States was through this sign language interpreter in the little bubble on the right side of the screen interpreting a sermon delivered by a Baptist minister.

I continued to be exposed to the deaf community at the schools I attended. As a hearing student in public schools during the 1970s and 1980s, I sat in classes experiencing the results of Public Law 94-142 (Education for All Handicapped Children Act, now called Individuals with Disabilities Education Act [IDEA]), which was passed by Congress in 1975. In order to receive federal funding, schools were required by law to develop and implement policies that would ensure a free and appropriate public education to all children with disabilities. For many deaf and hard of hearing students this meant attempts at mainstreaming, which were often unsuccessful: "The idea of 'integrating the handicapped' with the larger population has an inherent attraction, but the mainstreaming movement has caused disruptions in the education of deaf children."[1] Since its inception, mainstreaming has taken on a variety of appearances in public schools. In some schools, a single deaf student sitting in the front row of a classroom trying to read the teacher's lips was considered a mainstreaming program. In other public schools, more elaborate systems were created to include multiple deaf students in classes with an interpreter sitting in the front of the classroom and signing all verbal communications.

I attended mainstreamed schools that housed the programs for all deaf students and students with hearing loss in southeast Los Angeles County (the program was referred to as SELACO). At these schools, deaf students, often in clusters of threes, sat in the front rows of math, science, and occasionally history or geography classes. One interpreter sat off to the side in the front of the class, signing for the teacher and voicing for the deaf students. I never saw deaf students in English classes, which I assumed were held separately from the classes for hearing students. At the schools I attended, mainstreaming did not mean the deaf and hearing students were together in every class for every subject. Deaf students may have had language and English classes separate from hearing language and English classes. These campuses had temporary buildings that housed the SELACO program. Offices, classrooms, and open areas were set up in these "trailers." Because I attended mainstreamed schools, I was allowed to take sign language classes as elective credits as early as the sixth grade (the other schools in our district did not offer sign language classes). A few of my friends and I took sign language classes in junior high school so that we could better communicate with the SELACO students in our classes (and "talk" with each other in class without making noise and getting in trouble). As part of the sign language classes, we often visited the trailers to "perform" songs in sign language for the deaf students and their teachers and interpreters. At that time I didn't know about or understand all of the educational and sociological complexities involved in mainstreaming. I just knew that throughout junior high school and high school I could communicate with the deaf students in my math classes with the little bit of sign language I had learned in the sixth grade.[2]

Mainstreaming has been criticized for many reasons. Some people have argued that when PL 94-142 was passed, money and students were taken away from state residential schools that served deaf students: "Within a decade under this law, residential schools that had once enrolled as many as five hundred children found themselves with as few as one hundred and fifty."[3] Fewer state funds for residential programs of course meant fewer students attending residential schools. Besides its economic impact, mainstreaming has also been criticized for having a sociological impact on the deaf community. Deaf students attending public schools may not interact with any other deaf individuals, especially deaf adults who could become role models or mentors. Mainstreamed deaf students may never learn about Deaf culture, including American Sign Language (ASL), a key marker of the Deaf culture in the United States. As theories of educating deaf children have evolved, many mainstreaming programs have come to incorporate an introduction to Deaf culture. A bilingual-bicultural approach to educating deaf children does not ignore the language and culture of Deaf people as many mainstreaming programs do. In fact, schools should reinforce a positive deaf identity by offering students an educational system that is both bilingual and bicultural.[4] Such a program would require more involvement from the deaf community in the education of deaf children, but "at present, its role . . . is minimal."[5] This is in contrast to historical evidence that demonstrates that it was through the involvement of deaf educators, ministers, and leaders that a deaf community emerged.

My early introduction to the deaf community in the United States connected religious rhetoric with sign language. Little did I know that many years later I would examine the use of religious rhetoric by members of the deaf community to preserve and support sign language, and thus the deaf community. At this point I would like to clarify some of the terms I use throughout this book. The phrase "deaf community" refers not only to Deaf people—those who have a physical hearing loss, use American Sign Language, and share common cultural values, traditions, and social patterns—but also to hearing participants, such as friends or relatives, and to deaf people (those who have a physical hearing loss but perhaps do not subscribe to the values of Deaf culture) who are active in the community. The term "deaf community" encompasses a larger population than Deaf culture. I am using the terms "deaf community" and "Deaf culture," not "Deaf community"; therefore, people who may not be Deaf are still members of the larger community. Lowercase deaf refers to people who do not identify as culturally Deaf. In much scholarship that focuses on the deaf community and Deaf culture, the distinction of "lowercase d" and "capital D" is often made along similar lines.

I argue that religion has provided the deaf community with a powerful language to convey its authority in its struggles to preserve sign language. For this book, I define "rhetoric" as the use of language—oral or signed—to influence the thoughts and behaviors of individuals or groups. Religious rhetoric is then the use of language that has the features of religious themes, metaphors, and biblical references to influence the thoughts and behaviors of audiences. The examples of religious rhetoric explored in this project are products of an evangelical Protestant belief system, or Christian theology, grounded in the gospels. The main works I analyze are sermons and speeches of deaf community leaders and narratives of deaf community members. These works are historical and contemporary, sacred and secular, collected from Gallaudet University's archives and published sources. I show that the deaf community in the United States has employed religious rhetoric to overcome the oppression of a dominant hearing community that suppressed the use of sign language or that continues to misunderstand the value of sign language to the deaf community.

As a foundation for the use of religious rhetoric by the deaf community, I present in chapter 1 an analysis of Thomas Hopkins Gallaudet's use of religious rhetoric in the opening address of the first school for deaf students in the United States. My analysis shows the intersection of education for deaf Americans and Protestant missionary efforts to convert the deaf students. Through religious rhetoric, Gallaudet, who was hearing, constructed arguments for the education of a group of people who would later be identified as a deaf community and were most recognizable by their use of sign language. Before examining Gallaudet's sermon, I review contemporary scholarship in deaf studies that alludes to the connection between the deaf community in the United States and Protestantism, mainly through education. My work builds on this scholarship by exploring the continued use of religious rhetoric by the deaf community to support sign language. I also review some recent scholarship in rhetoric by Roxanne Mountford, Beth Daniell, and Carol Mattingly, which focuses on other contexts for religious rhetoric. My work contributes to this new scholarship by locating religious rhetoric, which is often disregarded, within the deaf community.

In the second chapter I explore the religious rhetoric found in deaf educators' speeches, school curricula, school brochures, and deaf community members' arguments in support of the use of sign language. Historically, Protestant ministers influenced the lives and worship choices of the deaf students they served on residential school campuses. As chapel services at residential schools became less frequent and requirements to attend them declined, students began making their own choices about religious beliefs and practices. Deaf students often based their choices on language use and their preference for sign language. By examining the religious rhetoric associated with residential schools of the past, I argue that these schools constituted a significant location where Protestant theology was intertwined with arguments for sign language. Pedagogical methods for the education of deaf students divided the manualists and the oralists, both of whom used evidence from their differing ideologies to support their arguments. The manualists argued that sign language was a gift from God, whereas the oralists argued that hand gestures, such as sign language, were more animal-like and thus an example of less development on the evolutionary scale.

In chapter 3 I extend the discussions of Douglas Baynton and Susan Burch regarding the sanctuary as a foundation for the key qualities that identify the deaf community: sign language and social groups. Sign language flourished in churches, and members of the deaf community formed relationships there. This chapter explores the religious rhetoric of ministers to the deaf community who played a significant part in the preservation of sign language. It builds on the previous chapter by examining the sanctuary as a location where religious rhetoric is used to advocate for the use and preservation of sign language by the deaf community in the United States.

The fourth chapter examines social activism and advocacy within the deaf community. I focus on two significant examples of deaf activism: the use of films by the National Association of the Deaf (NAD) in the early twentieth century to advocate for the preservation of sign language and Deaf West Theatre's twenty-first-century production of *Big River: The Adventures of Huckleberry Finn.* The NAD films use religious rhetoric to advocate for the preservation of sign language, and Deaf West uses it to support the recognition and acceptance of sign language and the deaf community. Historically, the deaf community had no way to preserve its language and heritage until the advent of film. Beginning in 1913 George Veditz led the NAD in a political attempt to preserve sign language by recording signed speeches and stories on film.[6] By producing films of master signers, Veditz intended to influence a new generation of signers who maintained the beauty and grace of the language. These films, usually containing religious themes and rhetoric, were also intended to promote hearing Americans to advocate for the preservation of sign language. Veditz wanted hearing audiences to see and understand the value of signs as language and therefore help preserve the use of sign language. Throughout the twentieth century, the deaf community continued to advocate for sign language use and access to information. Its members gained access to telecommunication through TTY and to films and television programs through the provision of captions. They were *heard* through the Deaf President Now protest of 1988. However, it is a theater production from 2004 that clearly demonstrates a new form of advocacy by the deaf community. One production blurring cultural boundaries is Deaf West Theatre's production of *Big River: The Adventures of Huckleberry Finn.* This musical uses both hearing and deaf actors signing and singing together. In discussing the musical's many spiritual references, the choices made with regard to how to execute certain signs, and the production's impact on mainstream theater,[7] I show that *Big River* is significant to the deaf community's empowered offensive stance. Deaf West's production aims to move audiences to accept and recognize the value of sign language. This chapter establishes the role of religious rhetoric in sacred and secular contexts of activism in the deaf community.

In the concluding chapter, I discuss the implications of the American deaf community's use of religious rhetoric on a deaf identity that values sign language. Since sign language is one key marker of the deaf community, advancements in technology offering deaf individuals opportunities to alleviate their deafness and thus their need for sign language have complicated what it means to be D/deaf. Because of assistive technology, more deaf and hard of hearing students enter the postsecondary writing classroom, where they must deal with issues of identity through their use of language. I offer suggestions for further research and study in this area, arguing for more work to be done with contemporary members of the deaf community in the United States, specifically with deaf and hard of hearing students in the predominantly hearing writing classroom, as well as research that examines international deaf communities.

Notes

1. Padden and Humphries, *Deaf in America,* 115.

2. Later in life I returned to studying sign language and Deaf culture and earned a certificate in sign language education. I have done extensive interpreting of religious services. But the most exciting interpreting experience I have ever had was providing sign language interpreting at a town hall meeting for President Barack Obama and Vice President Joe Biden in 2010.

3. Padden and Humphries, *Deaf in America,* 116.

4. Kannapell, *Language Choice Reflects Identity Choice,* 302.

5. Ibid., 306.

6. Burch, "Capturing a Movement," 294.

7. *Big River: The Adventures of Huckleberry Finn* received two 2003 Tony nominations for best revival of a musical and best performance by a featured actor in a musical. *Big River* also went on a national/international tour in 2004.

1

Intersections of Deafness, Religion, and Rhetoric

To BETTER explore the intersections of deafness, religion, and rhetoric, I need to explore what those who have come before me have examined near these intersections. My project examines the intersections of all three of these in the locations of schools, the sanctuary, and the social activism of deaf people. However, much has not been written on these with respect to rhetorical studies, which is what my project offers.

Deaf Studies: Education and Religion

Many contemporary deaf studies scholars have explored the history of deaf education in the United States.[1] While some works focus more on the inception of deaf education, others have focused on the debates over the use of sign language.[2] However, the analysis of the religious rhetoric used by members of the deaf community to argue for the preservation of sign language is not prominently featured in these works and does not offer any contemporary examples of such rhetoric. Much of the recent scholarship that has focused on contemporary issues in the deaf community examines the debates regarding methods of educating deaf students (e.g., mainstreaming; immersion; bilingual-bicultural teaching environments).[3] Some well-known works imply a connection between religion and deaf education but mainly explore the reasons that "[h]earing society in the U.S. has been slow to give up the idea of Deaf people as pathological handicapped individuals."[4]

Some works in deaf studies have alluded to the historical intersection of deaf education and faith. Many works acknowledge Thomas Hopkins Gallaudet's role as a minister who helped lead the way for a school for deaf students in the United States.[5] Others point out that the "nature and quality of instruction for the education of deaf individuals has been shaped by common behavioral attitudes and ideals" and that those attitudes and principles are "in harmony with Benedictine ideals."[6] Although Daniels claims that Gallaudet believed in the intelligence of deaf people, she does not explain how his role as a *Protestant* minister influenced his role as an educator. Her claim is that, like many educators of deaf students who came before him—Pedro Ponce de León, Juan Pablo Bonet, and Charles Michel de l'Epée—Gallaudet was a man of faith who valued the language and needs of deaf people. However, I argue, it was Gallaudet's Congregational, not Catholic, convictions that shaped him as a benevolent educator, a distinction Daniels does not make. I contend that Gallaudet's belief that deaf people have a right to be educated and learn their own language was directly related to his *evangelical* Protestant theology.

The following explanation of "evangelicalism" helps us to better understand the theology that influenced Gallaudet:

> The most serviceable general definition for this modern evangelicalism has been provided by the British historian David W. Bebbington. It stresses four characteristics: biblicalism (or reliance on the Bible as ultimate religious authority), conversionism (or an emphasis on the new birth), activism (or energetic, individualistic engagement in personal and social duties), and crucicentrism (or focus on Christ's redeeming work as the heart of true religion).[7]

As a Protestant minister, Gallaudet subscribed to this evangelicalism. Believing that the gospels of the Bible were true, Gallaudet relied on his own reading and interpretation of the Bible rather than on intercession with papal authority. For Gallaudet, it was *his* duty as a servant of God to teach and convert others. This assessment of Gallaudet's Protestant influence is in line with his education at Andover Theological Seminary, which stressed the importance of "spreading the gospel."[8] For Gallaudet, deaf people were lost souls who needed to be taught the importance of the Bible and the gospel message of Christ's birth, death, and resurrection. Gallaudet wanted to convert deaf Americans through a common language of signs that they would learn at the first permanent school for deaf people. Through this sign language, Gallaudet believed, deaf individuals would be able to individually rely on the Bible.

Like Daniels, many scholars acknowledge the presence of the Protestant religion at the founding of the American School for the Deaf, which took place in Connecticut in 1817, but they do not examine in depth the impact of this presence on the deaf community. Therefore, I examine this school as one of the intersections of deafness, rhetoric, and religion.

One significant influence of Protestant religion on deaf education that is highlighted in several studies is the historical role of religion, through deaf church leaders and ministries, in the survival of sign language. Historian Susan Burch maintains that "Deaf religious organizations commanded attention at conferences and in Deaf periodicals, and provided a source of considerable cultural pride for Deaf people."[9] At Deaf churches or state school chapels, the sanctuary became a place where signing flourished even in the middle of debates on oralism.[10] Historian Douglas C. Baynton contends that religion played a significant role in these debates. He claims that, although there were similarities between the oralists' and manualists' views of deaf people as outsiders, they divided by secular and Christian beliefs ideologically.[11] For oralists, the deaf community threatened a unified national identity: "Oralists likened the deaf community to a community of immigrants. They charged that the use of sign language encouraged deaf people to associate principally with each other and to avoid the hard work of learning to communicate in spoken English."[12] Oralists charged that "no gesturer [could] become an American"[13] until the person evolved beyond gestural language. For oralists, sign language use equated to a lower stature, a lower class, or an outsider status. On the other hand, manualists often argued that gestural language came before speech. For some evangelical Protestants, the biblical account of the creation of humankind was interpreted to suggest

> that God had originally given humans the capacity for language and had left them to develop that capacity themselves over time. Of those who believed that language developed over time, many argued that some form of gesture or sign language must have been used before spoken language. . . . To the manualist generation, "original language" meant "closer to the Creation."[14]

According to Baynton, manualists viewed the use of sign language as a way of demonstrating a deaf person's closeness to God. Baynton's work, like Burch's, is important because it highlights the role religion played in an aspect of life for the deaf community of early America. Specifically, Baynton's work demonstrates that religious rhetoric was used among manualists to debate their stance on deaf education. His research is invaluable for understanding the ideological differences between the manualists and the oralists and suggests the importance of focusing on the role of religion in sign language advocacy and of studying the continuing role of religious rhetoric in the deaf community.

Rhetorical Studies: Religion and Deafness

Deafness presents silence in rhetoric in two ways. First, the lack of rhetorical scholarship on the deaf community's use of rhetoric itself constitutes a silence in our field. Second, because among the varied definitions of rhetoric is the idea that a rhetor uses speech to persuade a listening audience, deaf audiences' lack of hearing and deaf rhetors' lack of oral performance create a silent rhetoric. In fact, Brenda Jo Brueggemann refers to deafness as "a thorn in rhetoric's side" because of the silence deafness creates.[15] Her work examines how rhetoric is used to construct deafness. Since rhetoric is about the power of language to change an audience's thoughts and behaviors, the deaf community was often disempowered by a dominant hearing community that was unfamiliar with sign language. In this book I explore the deaf community's use of religious metaphors and references familiar to both hearing and deaf audiences to advocate for the preservation and use of sign language.

Religion plays an important part in the history of many Americans. But, for the most part, religion has been widely ignored in the scholarship of the humanities. In various works in rhetorical studies, we see scholars turning attention to religious locations and religious rhetoric.[16] In the field of rhetoric, there have been few significant publications that remind us that the importance of religion and spiritual matters in general is tied to the life experiences of many Americans. In her work, Roxanne Mountford explores contemporary women preachers in the context of traditionally masculine, Protestant rhetorical space,[17] while Beth Daniell investigates an often overlooked population that reads and writes for spiritual development. She reminds her readers that spiritual experiences are significant to many individuals, like the five Mountain City women highlighted in her project.[18] Carol Mattingly explores the use of religious rhetoric by women, specifically claiming that despite their presence as the largest group of women rhetors and orators of the nineteenth century, temperance women have not been given critical attention by contemporary rhetorical scholars.[19]

These three works have had a significant impact on my project by leading me to the intersection of religion and rhetorical studies.

The location of Mountford's work is the sanctuary, and much of the evidence she analyzes comprises sermons and other religious rhetoric. Recognizing the significance of religion to studies in rhetoric, I would like to add to the tradition of Mountford's scholarship by exploring the cultural connection between religion and the American deaf community's discourse related to the advocacy of sign language, especially in the location of the sanctuary.

For many communities, religion or spirituality is a significant bond holding the members together. Daniell's work explores the intersection of religion and literacy. In her first chapter, she recounts the experience of hearing Ann Berthoff at the Conference on College Composition and Communication, where Berthoff explained "that Paulo Freire's pedagogy of the oppressed comes not just from his Marxism but from his Catholicism as well."[20] Influenced by the connection between Freire's work and theology, Daniell suggests that literacy work can tap into something beyond the student, the teacher, and the reader.[21] Like the women in Daniell's study, deaf Americans of the early nineteenth century formed a community through their use of language and their literacy practices. Their literacy was directly tied to Gallaudet's Protestant theology. Gallaudet's mission was that the first school for the deaf in the United States would serve to centralize sign language and provide students with a way through that language to individually come to know God.

Carol Mattingly claims that "evangelical women created their own standards for Christianity, which they deliberately delineated from orthodox patriarchal religious organizations. Their own interpretation of Christian principles and their appeal to a 'higher authority' justified their defiance of patriarchal authority and enabled them to demand greater rights for women."[22] Through critical analysis of the rhetoric of temperance women that she gathered from personal writings, fiction, newspapers, and meeting minutes, Mattingly offers a voice for a religious population that has been ignored in the field of rhetoric. More important, she explains how the Protestant theology subscribed to by the temperance women influenced their reliance on the Bible and therefore their arguments. Like Mattingly, I, too, offer the field of rhetoric a study of an often silenced population that uses religious rhetoric to make itself visible.

As the deaf community struggled to maintain and preserve its language, its members engaged the rich sources of Protestant rhetoric. In the nineteenth and early twentieth centuries, the American deaf community's use of religious rhetoric empowered its arguments by connecting with a dominant hearing community of like-minded believers. More recently, religious rhetoric used in the deaf community has been fostered to bolster the resolve of deaf community members to continue to preserve sign language and to convince audiences in secular settings to sympathize with the plight of the deaf community and support the use and recognition of sign language.

Protestant Leaders, Deaf Education, and Religious Rhetoric: Building a Foundation for the Deaf Community

Protestant leaders in the deaf community have been instrumental in the preservation of sign language. To study elements of the deaf community in the United States one must acknowledge the history of the education of deaf students. It is because of schools like the American School for the Deaf that deaf Americans began to socialize with each other by forming relationships, clubs, organizations, and churches. As John Vickery Van Cleve and Barry A. Crouch note, "[u]ltimately, schools brought deaf people together, forming a context within which they would develop their own cultural communities."[23] Schools were a venue in which deaf students learned and used sign language. Once schools opened up for deaf students, they, too, became a location where deaf individuals could meet other deaf individuals, often for the first time. Christopher Krentz states that "[i]n 1818, [Laurent] Clerc wrote that of forty-two students at the American Asylum, only 'four or six' had met other deaf people before coming to Hartford."[24] Education of deaf people in the United States offered opportunities for deaf individuals to bond and then to form a community based on a common language. Because the first school for deaf people in the United States was grounded in Gallaudet's Protestant theology, to examine the history of deaf education is to clearly see an intertwining of religious and general instruction.

As a minister, Gallaudet garnered support for the American School for the Deaf by persuading his audience that the souls of deaf people needed to be saved, the core of his evangelical Protestant theology. He employed religious themes to argue for the teaching of sign language. He argued that sign language should be taught to deaf students, that deaf students should be taught in sign language, and that sign language would give the deaf students an understanding of "the influences of the Spirit" and an "understanding of the Author of [their] being."[25] Gallaudet's Protestant beliefs, combined with Clerc's strong Catholic background, became the cornerstones of the American School for the Deaf. Gallaudet wanted to save souls, while Clerc's faith inspired him to educate deaf people to fulfill "the needs of the state" and "the temporal needs of the individual," as well as for "justice" and "the fraternity of man (which includes education)."[26] Clerc was motivated to give deaf people a language so they could "illuminate their lives" on their own.[27] Gallaudet wanted to enlighten the lives of deaf students himself. These men worked together to provide deaf Americans a place to learn sign language and to acquire an education with a curriculum grounded in Gallaudet's Protestant beliefs.

Before Gallaudet, there were many educators of deaf people. Like Gallaudet, many of them saw their work as service to God. One of the earliest records of a sign system used for communicating with deaf people is that of a sixteenth-century Spanish monk, Fray Melchor de Yebra.[28] In the seventeenth century, Europe was influenced by Spain's success in educating the deaf children of noble families.[29] In England, books were published on how to educate deaf children, and educators soon began to cater to the deaf children of wealthy parents.[30] But it was in the eighteenth century that European schools for deaf children began to open. Some, like the Royal Institution for the Deaf in Paris, endorsed the manual method, while others emerged using a strictly oralist approach. Van Cleve and Crouch note that "[f]oremost among these were German schools that followed the oralist pattern established by an eighteenth-century teacher, Samuel Heinicke. In the nineteenth century oralism . . . was usually called the German method."[31] These early European schools, as well as the Braidwood Academy in Scotland, influenced the deaf educational system in the United States. These two pedagogical approaches—manual versus oral—were philosophically opposed and set the stage for a long debate that continues today.[32]

The Braidwood Academy was an oral school that attempted to help deaf students to master speech and thus, in its view, to acquire the ability to reason.[33] Some wealthy American parents sent their deaf children to the academy, hoping they would return home able to speak, understand, and reason in English. The most well-known case of such a family is the Bollings who in 1770 sent all of their children to the Braidwood Academy in Scotland. The success of the Braidwood Academy led to the founding of more schools throughout England, but the Braidwood family was unsuccessful in establishing a school in the United States. Plagued with personal problems—drinking, gambling, and debt—John Braidwood, grandson of the founder of Braidwood Academy, ended up in jail rather than opening a school in the United States.[34]

In contrast to the Braidwood Academy, the Abbé Charles-Michel de l'Epée at the Royal Institution for the Deaf in Paris taught deaf students using a sign system. As an educator, de l'Epée was "[u]nlike anyone before him . . . [and] took as his goal to give many deaf children some knowledge of language, albeit silent, rather than giving a small number a mastery of speech."[35] By encouraging deaf students to use their own language, de l'Epée was perhaps allowing a deaf community with its own language to emerge, unlike the Braidwood Academy, which tried to teach deaf students to act hearing by using speech and lipreading. De l'Epée's successful teaching methods were passed on to his successor, the Abbé Roch-Ambroise Sicard. As the head of the Royal Institution for the Deaf, Sicard took former students to London, where they demonstrated their accomplishments for many people, including Gallaudet.

Suffering from a physical condition that diminished his stamina, Gallaudet became a minister after pursuing a career in business. After graduating from Yale in 1805, for a short while he studied law and English literature and composition before returning to Yale, where he received a master of arts degree in 1810.[36] While studying theology at Andover Seminary from 1812 to 1814, Gallaudet visited home during breaks from his studies. On one such visit he met Alice Cogswell, the deaf daughter of a neighbor. Because of his physical condition, Gallaudet did not often run and play with his siblings while they were growing up. He may have identified with Alice, whom he saw playing alone. The well-known story is that he tried communicating with her by writing in the dirt. Alice did not know written English, so Gallaudet taught her the word "hat" by laying his hat down and then spelling *h-a-t* in the dirt. Motivated by this interaction, Gallaudet wanted to make sure Alice had a language.

Dr. Mason Fitch Cogswell, Alice's father, solicited a group of Congregational clergymen to take a census of deaf children in Connecticut.[37] Cogswell did not want to send Alice to school in Europe, which at the time was the only educational option for her since there were no schools for deaf children in the United States. This census pointed out the need for a school to educate deaf individuals in the United States: The information they gathered

Thomas Hopkins Gallaudet. (Gallaudet University Archives, Washington, DC)

indicated that more than two thousand deaf individuals of educable age were living in the United States.[38] Cogswell, leading businessmen, and clergymen in Hartford gathered on April 13, 1815, to discuss the establishment of a school for deaf students in the United States. These men believed they had a divine purpose, and at their initial meeting "they began with an invocation of God's blessing on the undertaking by Rev. Strong, minister of the first church of Hartford."[39] As a result of their gatherings, they asked Gallaudet to go to Europe to learn techniques to educate deaf children.

While in London, Gallaudet attended Sicard's demonstration, and there he saw Laurent Clerc, a former student and current teacher at the Royal Institution. Sicard invited Gallaudet to visit the school, and after several months he returned to the United States with Clerc. On the trip home, Gallaudet worked with Clerc to improve his English, and Clerc began teaching Gallaudet sign language.[40] Both men were embarking on what they thought of as a mission to do God's will. Sicard referred to Clerc as "the Apostle of the Deaf-Mutes of the New World," and Clerc accepted his journey to the United States as his fulfillment of a calling by God.[41]

At the heart of Gallaudet's efforts to educate and give a language to deaf people in the United States was his mission to proselytize deaf people there and to convert them to Protestantism. As a graduate of Andover Seminary, which employed "a curriculum of biblical, systematic, historical, and practical theology designed for students who had completed a collegiate course in the liberal arts," Gallaudet was in a class of students who pursued mission fields around the world to spread their faith.[42] Andover Seminary was founded in 1808 as a Congregational seminary in response to the prevalence of Unitarianism. As a Trinitarian seminary, Andover taught evangelical theology grounded in the belief in the Trinity.[43]

Andover emerged during the Second Great Awakening, which extended from the late eighteenth century to the mid-nineteenth

Laurent Clerc. (Portrait by Charles Willson Peale, The American School for the Deaf, Hartford, CT)

century and left "permanent organizations designed to evangelize and reform America."[44] In 1810, Andover Seminary student Samuel J. Mills Jr. established the American Board of Commissioners for Foreign Missions.[45] These traveling evangelists were called missionaries, those who "took the gospel abroad," and the first American missionaries were sent to India and the Far East.[46] However, for many Protestant ministers "the work done by those who stayed at home to evangelize and civilize America was *the* truly great missionary story of the century."[47] For Gallaudet, the deaf community was a mission field, and education through sign language was a method for proselytizing deaf people. Protestantism influenced Gallaudet's motives for educating deaf Americans. Part of his theological grounding was rooted in his evangelical Protestantism:

> Evangelicals called people to acknowledge their sin before God, to look upon Jesus Christ (crucified—dead—resurrected) as God's means of redemption, and to exercise faith in this Redeemer as the way of reconciliation with God and orientation for life in the world. To evangelicals, the message was validated by their own experience of God's grace, but even more by its centrality in the Bible, which they held to be a unique revelation from God.[48]

Gallaudet sought to give sign language to deaf Americans so they would be able to understand the gospels and come to know God's grace. He served the function of minister to deaf students who had not been exposed to the gospels and of father or savior in the image of Christ, whom he emulated. Religion was thus intertwined with the learning of a sign language for oppressed outsiders, who later as a group embraced and grew under religion's influence.

Gallaudet's decision to proselytize unbelievers came before he discovered deaf people as his mission work. His decision, made at Cogswell's urging, to proselytize deaf Americans provided him a mission field in his homeland. Phyllis Valentine explains the setting that influenced Gallaudet's desire to do mission work:

> At Andover Seminary—a seedbed of evangelical Christian activity—Gallaudet had been fired with a desire to preach Christianity to the heathen. Many of his fellow seminarians established foreign missions in Hawaii, Africa, and Asia, and Reverend Gallaudet sometimes officiated at ceremonies marking their leave-taking, while he himself chose to stay closer to home. Nonetheless, he believed he was bound

> by the same injunction from Christ as his far-flung colleagues to convey the news of salvation to every creature on earth. As principal of the American Asylum, Gallaudet envisioned himself a missionary to "heathen" deaf people who had never before heard the Christian message of salvation.[49]

Like his colleagues entering foreign cultures, Gallaudet wanted to proselytize to deaf Americans who had never been exposed to the gospels in a language of their own understanding. For Gallaudet, deaf Americans were like the heathens in faraway lands because they were unconverted and did not know Christ. Once Gallaudet recognized them as his mission work, he had to garner support from the citizens of Connecticut.

Through the use of religious rhetoric, Gallaudet effectively conveyed the ideology of the community who was his audience. In May 1815, on the eve of his departure to Europe, Gallaudet delivered an address to a group of Hartford citizens. He convinced them that his mission work was significant and had been neglected by the United States. Referring to deaf people in the United States, Gallaudet argued, "[t]heir *numbers;* their *condition;* and the *practicability* of affording them relief address loud claims to every feeling heart."[50] Gallaudet supported his argument by citing information in the census taken by the clergymen in Connecticut. The benefits that deaf people would receive from gaining a language and acquiring an education were great, Gallaudet claimed. He asserted that deaf Europeans had been taught "to not only read and write and understand written language with accuracy, but, in some cases, to understand spoken language, and to speak themselves audibly and intelligibly."[51] He tried to persuade his audience that deaf Americans could also be taught to read and write, but, more important, they could come to know God:

> Now if the deaf and dumb in our country can by a proper course of instruction be fitted for useful and respectable employments in life; if they can have their minds opened to the reception of such intellectual

> and moral improvement as will render them comfortable and happy on this side of the grave, above all if they can be made acquainted with the revelation of God's mercy through Jesus Christ, who can hesitate to promote an object which is pregnant with so much good, and which addresses itself to the most enlarged views of Christian benevolence.[52]

Gallaudet preached to an audience of predominantly like-minded Christians, for "Protestant evangelicals . . . came to dominate religious life in the early Unites States [sharing] an emphasis on conversions, the supreme religious authority of the Bible, and an active life of personal holiness."[53] Gallaudet's goals for educating deaf Americans were centered on his effort to provide them with the knowledge that would lead them to spiritual salvation, echoing the value of middle-class citizens of Hartford, who would offer their financial and prayerful support.[54]

Gallaudet took the podium on April 20, 1817, at the opening assembly for the Connecticut Asylum for the Education and Instruction of Deaf and Dumb Persons (later the American School for the Deaf). The central text for his sermon was Isaiah 35:5–6: "Then the eyes of the blind shall be opened, and the ears of the deaf shall be unstopped. Then shall the lame man leap as an hart, and the tongue of the dumb sing: for in the wilderness shall waters break out, and streams in the desert."[55] Gallaudet began by acknowledging God's power to open the ears of deaf people and loosen the tongues of those who were mute.[56] He quickly moved to the justification for the school that he would be leading, assuming his own power to give the "deaf and dumb," or "lower creation," a language of their own and, with such language, a knowledge of Christ so they could be converted.[57] Gallaudet's reference to deaf people as "lower creation" was a reflection of his paternalism, which was grounded in both his social status and his Christian beliefs. Those who did not know God, Christians believed, were unfortunate. Gallaudet regarded his position as principal of the new asylum as a ministry, a calling, and a practice of his Christian benevolence—reaching down to help those less fortunate than he.

As a Congregationalist, Gallaudet subscribed to the central evangelical tenet of benevolence.[58] His Protestant faith played a significant role in deaf education in nineteenth-century America and thus in the emerging deaf community and its use of sign language. It was through his evangelical convictions that this community gained a religious belief system that would provide them with "personal empowerment."[59] Noll explains the evolution of this sense of empowerment:

> American evangelicals also shared a conviction that true religion required an active experience of God, one leading necessarily to discipline. . . . [T]hose principles embodied a common evangelical conviction that the gospel entailed a search for public godliness as well as personal holiness. In sum, they believed that the Bible taught a message of rescue and deliverance, and that this message provided moral guidance, personal empowerment, and direction for self and society.[60]

Through Gallaudet's Protestant influences, the early American deaf community gained an education and advocacy for sign language that was intertwined with evangelical theology as practiced in the United States.

Along with Clerc and with the guidance of Sicard, who was influenced by de l'Epée, Gallaudet devised a curriculum that would introduce many deaf students to Christianity, which would allow them to reap the benefits of speech and hearing when they reached "the Redeemer's Kingdom."[61] Citizens of Hartford, along with deaf students and relatives, were in the audience as Gallaudet delivered his sermon at the opening of the American School for the Deaf. He claimed that the greatest advantage to educating deaf people would be benefits difficult for hearing people to understand: "The most important advantages, however, in the education of the deaf and dumb accrue to those who are the subjects of it, and these are advantages, which it is extremely difficult for those of us, who are in possession of all our faculties, duly to appreciate."[62] According to Gallaudet, the hearing members of the audience, who already had a language and religious conviction of their own, would not be able to understand the significance of acquiring sign language and through it an introduction to evangelical Protestant theology as the deaf students would. He compared the silence and thus the ignorance of deaf people to the dreariness of living in a dungeon: "He, who has always trod the soil, and breathed the air, of freedom, cannot sympathize with the feelings of ecstasy, which glow in the breast of him, who, having long been the tenant of some dreary dungeon is brought forth to the cheering influence of light and liberty."[63] Gallaudet emphasized the "ecstasy" felt once a deaf person was freed from the bondage of ignorance. He appealed to the audience's emotions since he wanted them to sponsor the school and help those less fortunate than they. By teaching the deaf students a sign language, Gallaudet claimed, he could lead them to understand "how [their] offences may be pardoned through the blood of the Saviour; how [their] affections may be purified through the influences of the Spirit; how [they] may at last gain victory over death, and triumph over the horrors of the grave."[64] He offered to teach the deaf students sign language and to conduct their religious and general instruction in sign language. Persuasively appealing to his audience's awareness of the Bible, Gallaudet stated that the "light and liberty" the deaf students would be brought into were not necessarily freedom from silence or freedom through language; however, it was the freedom one experienced when one believed in God.[65]

Gallaudet told the audience that the freedoms found in their Protestant beliefs were foreign to a deaf person, who had neither the language nor the intellect to comprehend the liberation made possible through the Protestant faith. Continuing the theme of imprisonment and freedom, Gallaudet stated the following:

> There are *chains* more galling than those of the dungeon—the immortal mind preying upon itself, and so imprisoned as not to be able to unfold its intellectual and moral powers, and to attain to the comprehension and enjoyment of those objects, which the Creator has designed as the sources of its highest expectations and hopes. Such must often be the condition of the uninstructed deaf and dumb![66]

According to Gallaudet, the path to a better life for deaf people would include religious training that opposed predestination and maintained that the deaf students would be able to come to know God personally. The ultimate benefit they would reap under Gallaudet's direction would be to know "the Saviour of their souls"—moving from the darkness of their "dungeons" into the light of God.[67] For Gallaudet, sign language would become the light to the school's deaf students, who were living in the dark. His use of religious rhetoric placed on the audience a responsibility for the immortal "souls" of the deaf students in their presence.

Identifying himself as a servant of God who was created in God's own image, Gallaudet challenged his audience:

> It is Jesus Christ whom we are *thus* bound to love, to imitate, and to obey. We are stewards, but of *his* vineyard. *Whatsoever* we do, should be done in *his* name. For it is by this *test*, that all our efforts to do good will be tried at the great day of his dread and awful retribution.[68]

Gallaudet called his audience to action and asserted that the standards he assumed for himself were to be found in his relationship to and faith in God. As believers, the audience had a part to play in Gallaudet's mission. They, too, should do the work of God and help to promote the conversions of the deaf students. They, too, should proselytize deaf people by supporting the deaf education movement in the United States, as those who are not called to foreign lands are to support Christian missionaries with prayers and gifts.

Gallaudet concluded his sermon with a call for humility. He reflected on all that his audience could do to help deaf people but added that their efforts would nonetheless be imperfect in comparison to what Christ would do for them in return. He also claimed that their reliance on Christ would allow them to do whatever was necessary to help the deaf students. By challenging the believers in his audience, as he had done earlier on the eve of his trip to Europe, Gallaudet expanded his mission field beyond the students he would witness to and train in religion to include the people of Hartford and potential supporters of the school. He reminded his audience to appreciate what they had been given and what deaf Americans were lacking. Appealing to the audience's sympathy, Gallaudet urged them to

> be grateful to God for the very superior advantages which *we* enjoy; consider how imperfectly we improve [deaf people]; be mindful, that after all we do, we are but unprofitable servants; and thus, feeling the necessity of our continual reliance upon Jesus Christ, trust alone to *his righteousness* for acceptance with God.[69]

At the close of his sermon, Gallaudet positioned himself (as well as the Christians in the audience) as superior to the deaf students who would be under his instruction, and he noted that the advantages he enjoyed came from God. Although there would be benefits to educating deaf Americans, Gallaudet's efforts to "improve them" would be imperfect without his reliance on God, for it was through God that he saw his work finished.[70]

The need to educate not only deaf people but also all outsiders about the American Christian belief in the gospels continued to be at the heart of Gallaudet's sermons. A few years after the opening of the American School for the Deaf, Gallaudet claimed, on October 11, 1819, that, "[i]f it was the duty of the primitive Christians, in compliance with the injunction of Christ, to send missionaries to enlighten *our ancestors* with the truths of the gospel, it is equally our duty to convey a knowledge of the same truths to the *present* heathen world."[71] Gallaudet explained to the audience that the evangelical duties they adhered to as Christians had not changed over time. Andover reinforced Gallaudet's conviction regarding missionary service. For him, deaf individuals were outsiders who needed to be brought into the flock and then to knowledge of God by means of sign language. He would thus be fulfilling a primary purpose of Andover—"a *learned* and *evangelical* ministry": spreading the gospel to a population who had not heard it.[72]

After a ceremony celebrating the marriage of a couple who had dedicated themselves to the Sandwich Mission,[73] Gallaudet referred to Paul as a hero when he left Ephesus to begin his missionary work. The Sandwich Islands were what we now call Hawaii. This couple made a decision to travel to the islands to live with the inhabitants and proselytize them.[74] Gallaudet respected and sympathized with the men and women who would leave their own country to proselytize in a foreign land but viewed their work, although emotionally draining, as nonetheless comforting because they were fulfilling an evangelical Protestant conviction that believers must become more like Christ:

> [The Christian missionary] follows the example of Jesus Christ. In his last hours of agony, while he yet hung a bleeding victim on the cross; enduring the severest tokens of his Father's displeasure against sin; his whole soul engaged in the completion of his mysterious work of love to our fallen race; and just ready to exclaim "it is finished;" his eye beheld the mother who bore him, and filial gratitude glowed in his breast.[75]

For Gallaudet, Christian missionaries endured many hardships that he compared to Christ's sacrifice; yet, he believed that they were comforted by the fact that their work answered a higher calling that paralleled Christ's example.

While Gallaudet acknowledged the work of missionaries to foreign lands, he also acknowledged the place of those who stayed home to help in the evangelical missions:

> And while most of us are not called to this arduous service, but permitted to remain at home in the bosom of civilized society, how grateful should we be to those who are willing to take their lives in their hands; to forsake friends and home and country, and to encounter the severest trials, that they may enable us, in some measure, to fulfill our obligations to our Saviour, while they only ask of us our good wishes, and prayers, and a portion of our charity.[76]

These descriptions of Gallaudet's feelings about missionary work demonstrate his belief that the call to save the "heathen" was an important duty. And despite not feeling called to foreign service himself, Gallaudet found his own mission work with "heathens" close to home. He was motivated to teach deaf students about God so that they could be converted. They enabled him to pursue his motivation to convert unbelievers, and he considered them similar to other non-Christians that evangelical missionaries were proselytizing abroad. It is important to note that missionary work is often viewed as colonizing communities and resulting in long-lasting changes to foreign cultures (e.g., the evangelizing and "Americanization" of many Native American tribes).[77] Gallaudet's missionary work with the deaf students near Hartford has in fact created long-lasting effects. His work included invoking religious rhetoric to influence a community to support a school for deaf people in the United States and ministering to deaf Americans through sign language.

As founders of the American School for the Deaf, Gallaudet and Clerc are often referred to as the fathers of deaf education in the United States. Gallaudet, a hearing minister, influenced Clerc, a deaf Catholic who later converted to Protestantism. Their strong religious examples inspired many deaf community leaders who came after them. Like Gallaudet and Clerc, superintendents and teachers at residential schools typically were educated for the ministry or in some cases left these schools to become ministers. For example, Olof Hanson, a deaf leader and community activist in the early twentieth century, became an Episcopal minister after careers in architecture and deaf education. For many students at these residential schools, the ministers who delivered the chapel services in sign language became Deaf role models and strongly shaped the students' moral behavior.[78] As deaf community leaders emerged in the twentieth century, many were either ministers or strongly involved in churches that ministered to the deaf community. They would have a strong impact on the intertwining of Protestantism and the deaf community's advocacy for sign language.

Gallaudet had a profound impact on deaf education in the United States. His use of religious rhetoric lent power to the view that the emerging deaf community was made up of intelligent human beings who deserved an opportunity to be educated through sign language in order to know God. Gallaudet's two sons, Edward Miner Gallaudet and the Reverend Thomas Gallaudet, continued their father's ministry by working with the deaf community in the areas of education and religion well into the early twentieth century.

Notes

1. See Lane, *When the Mind Hears;* Van Cleve and Crouch, *Place of Their Own;* Baynton, *Forbidden Signs;* and Burch, *Signs of Resistance.*
2. Winefield, *Never the Twain Shall Meet;* Baynton, *Forbidden Signs.*
3. See Ramsey, *Deaf Children in Public Schools.*
4. Woodward, *How You Gonna Get to Heaven,* 1.
5. See Lane, *When the Mind Hears;* Valentine, "Thomas Hopkins Gallaudet"; Crouch and Greenwald, "Hearing with the Eye"; Van Cleve and Crouch, *Place of Their Own.*
6. Daniels, *Benedictine Roots,* 97.
7. Noll, *America's God,* 5.
8. Noll, *History of Christianity,* 186.

9. Burch, "Biding the Time," 32.

10. The oral method of teaching encompassed the use of speech and lip-reading to communicate without the use of sign language.

11. See Baynton, *Forbidden Signs.*

12. Ibid., 16.

13. Ibid., 27.

14. Ibid., 39–40.

15. Brueggemann, *Lend Me Your Ears,* 2.

16. See Mountford, *Gendered Pulpit;* Daniell, *Communion of Friendship;* Mattingly, *Well-Tempered Women.*

17. See Mountford, *Gendered Pulpit.*

18. See Daniell, *Communion of Friendship.*

19. Mattingly, *Well-Tempered Women,* 1.

20. Daniell, *Communion of Friendship,* 19.

21. Ibid.

22. Mattingly, *Well-Tempered Women,* 8.

23. Van Cleve and Crouch, *Place of Their Own,* 10.

24. Krentz, *Mighty Change,* xvii.

25. Gallaudet, "Sermon Delivered at the Opening of the Connecticut Asylum," 9.

26. Lane, *When the Mind Hears,* 201, 204.

27. Ibid., 204.

28. Van Cleve and Crouch, *Place of Their Own,* 10; Beryl Lieff Benderly, *Dancing without Music,* 109; Lane, *When the Mind Hears,* 69; Daniels, *Benedictine Roots,* 11, 14.

29. Van Cleve and Crouch, *Place of Their Own,* 15; Benderly, *Dancing without Music,* 109; Lane, *When the Mind Hears,* 91–94; Daniels, *Benedictine Roots,* 29.

30. Benderly, *Dancing without Music,* 110; Lane, *When the Mind Hears,* 106.

31. Van Cleve and Crouch, *Place of Their Own,* 107.

32. This debate has been complicated in more recent times by emerging technologies such as cochlear implants.

33. Lane, *When the Mind Hears,* 106.

34. Van Cleve and Crouch, *Place of Their Own,* 25–26.

35. Benderly, *Dancing without Music,* 113.

36. Daniels, *Benedictine Roots,* 42.

37. Ibid., 43.

38. Ibid.

39. James John Fernandes, *Gate to Heaven,* 34.

40. Lane, *When the Mind Hears,* 206; Gannon, *Deaf Heritage,* xxiii.

41. Lane, *When the Mind Hears,* 203.

42. Noll, *America's God,* 254.
43. Ibid., 254, 260.
44. Noll, *History of Christianity,* 169.
45. Ibid., 186.
46. Ibid., 185.
47. Ibid.
48. Noll, *America's God,* 171.
49. Valentine, "Thomas Hopkins Gallaudet," 58–59.
50. Gallaudet, "Address to the Benevolent," 14. Emphasis in original.
51. Ibid.
52. Ibid.
53. Noll, *America's God,* 11.
54. Lane, *When the Mind Hears,* 229; Valentine, "Thomas Hopkins Gallaudet," 59–60.
55. Here I am quoting from the King James Version of the Bible, the same translation Gallaudet used for his sermon.
56. Gallaudet, "Sermon Delivered at the Opening," 4.
57. Ibid.
58. Noll, *America's God,* 178.
59. Ibid., 174.
60. Ibid.
61. Gallaudet, "Sermon Delivered at the Opening," 12.
62. Ibid., 7.
63. Ibid., 8.
64. Ibid., 9.
65. Here Gallaudet is referring to 2 Corinthians 3:17, which states that liberty is found in God: "Now the Lord is that Spirit: and where the Spirit of the Lord *is,* there *is* liberty" (KJV) (emphasis in original). Since deaf Americans had no language, Gallaudet believed, they were unable to know Jesus and experience the liberty he refers to in the preceding Bible passage. Gallaudet's subscription to evangelical Protestantism is apparent in that he finds freedom through his Christianity—or that "God has provided . . . salvation by grace" (Noll, *History of Christianity,* 46).
66. Gallaudet, "Sermon Delivered at the Opening," 8.
67. Ibid., 13.
68. Ibid., 12. Emphasis in original.
69. Ibid., 13. Emphasis in original.
70. Ibid.
71. Gallaudet, "Address Delivered at a Meeting," 10. Emphasis in original.
72. Pearson, "Historic Sketch," 7. Emphasis in original.
73. Gallaudet, "Sandwich Mission."
74. Ibid., 5.

75. Ibid., 7.
76. Ibid., 11.
77. See Noll, *History of Christianity*, 187.
78. Burch, *Signs of Resistance*, 46.

2

Protestant Ideology and the Arguments for Sign Language in Late Nineteenth-Century Schools for Deaf Children

I am proud to be a Deaf man, am very delighted with the divine gift *of ASL, and, indeed, enjoy reading texts in English.*

—Patrick A. Graybill, "Another New Birth" (emphasis added)

Deaf people often used biblical language to emphasize how the schools converted them from ignorance to knowledge, from isolation to community, from no language to ASL and English, and from heathenism to Christian redemption.

—Christopher Krentz, *A Mighty Change*

THE American School for the Deaf opened in 1817 with the initial mission to provide deaf students with a language and knowledge of God so they could be saved. As the previous chapter shows, Thomas Hopkins Gallaudet argued that teaching sign language to students and delivering the school's curriculum in sign language was the most effective way to achieve this goal. Appealing to audiences who held mainly Protestant beliefs, Gallaudet's speeches supporting sign language were often filled with biblical references and metaphors. His successes at the American School for the Deaf helped garner backing for deaf education nationally and influenced many other area schools not only to open but also to use sign language to teach deaf students. This method, known as *manualism*, was the primary means of teaching deaf students in the United States in the first half of the nineteenth century. In the latter half of the eighteen hundreds, the manualists' teaching practices, like those of Gallaudet, were

Edward Miner Gallaudet. (Gallaudet University Archives, Washington, DC)

challenged by educators who argued that deaf American students should learn to speak and read speech only, a practice known as *oralism*. In late nineteenth-century America, pure oralists did not want sign language to be used in schools for deaf students, which would have had the effect of eradicating the use of sign language completely. As the number of schools for deaf people in the

United States increased to serve an ever-growing population, the use of the oral method of instruction gained in popularity. Discussions on language use crept into debates on deaf education, causing some deaf community leaders to argue for the protection and continued use of what they called "the natural language of the deaf"—sign language. The arguments of late nineteenth-century manualists, who by this point were *combinists*,[1] continued to reflect the use of religious themes and references, much as Gallaudet's arguments had done in the early half of the nineteenth century.

Such arguments show that both practitioners and supporters of sign language used Protestant ideology. "Pure manualism" was the use of sign language only, without any instruction borrowed from oral approaches. However, by the latter half of the nineteenth century, many schools that were traditionally manual were incorporating oral approaches to instruction for some students who would benefit from them—especially those students who had recently become deaf and still had some or all of their ability to speak. This practice of using both the manual and the oral approach was known as the "combined method." Educators' arguments in favor of the combined method or the preservation of sign language were often evident in the *American Annals of the Deaf*, which was first published in 1847 and focused on deaf education. Both oralists and manualists, as well as those who became combinists, subscribed to and published in the *Annals*. I focus here on publications by the son of Thomas Hopkins Gallaudet, Edward Miner Gallaudet, who argued in the *Annals* for a combined system of instruction that employed the best practices of both oralism and manualism. Like his father, Edward Gallaudet made use of religious themes and references in his advocacy. He is also one of the most recognized leaders of the deaf community in the latter half of the nineteenth century because of his assistance to it and his endorsement of the use of sign language. His efforts culminated in the opening of the Collegiate Department of the

Columbia Institution for the Deaf and Dumb, later named after his father, in 1864.

The biblical language used in the arguments for sign language by deaf community leaders such as E. M. Gallaudet and Philip J. Hasenstab, an instructor at the Illinois Institution for the Deaf and Dumb, reflects the worldview of those who valued the use of sign language, a perspective that continued to find its way into deaf education. Thus, the Protestant ideology that began with T. H. Gallaudet's curriculum and pedagogy in the first permanent school for deaf students in the United States continued to surface in late nineteenth-century arguments for sign language use and even emerged in early twentieth-century school publications.

Late Nineteenth-Century Methods of Teaching Deaf Students

In the United States, more and more schools for deaf students opened in the late nineteenth century, but the educators who ran them did not agree on teaching methods. Some of them even argued for the end of sign language use. More opponents of sign language and manualist instruction methods emerged in the latter half of the nineteenth century. Very few oralists (i.e., those who believed that the best means of teaching deaf students was with no sign language) started making noise prior to 1850; however, later in that century, through suggestions at conferences and in presentations and publications, the oral method of instruction was touted by many as superior to the manual method. Early evidence of the oralists' arguments surfaced in Horace Mann's effort to challenge the use of sign language in the education of deaf students. In the 1840s, Mann, influenced by the oral methods used in Germany, argued for educational reform.[2]

In an 1848 article, Lewis Weld refers to the 1844 conversation occurring about possible advancements in the instruction of deaf people by Europeans who were using the oral method. Like Mann, Weld had traveled to Europe to observe the teaching practices there. He was the principal of the American School for the Deaf at this time and hoped to bring back a number of improvements in teaching methods.[3] Weld summed up his observations by stating "that whatever improvements had been made in those institutions during the previous twenty-seven years, they had not surpassed, if they had equalled, [*sic*] those of our own American institutions."[4] He disagreed with Mann that the oral methods they had both witnessed in Germany were superior to the manual methods the U.S. schools were still using. However, between Weld's European visit in 1844 and his "American Asylum" article in 1847, a change in instruction methods occurred in the U.S. institutions. In that article he mentions what may have marked the beginning of the combined method at the American School for the Deaf: a successful shift in emphasizing "articulation and reading on the lips" for those students who lost their hearing after they had learned to speak.[5] For Weld and for the American School for the Deaf, sign language was still the optimal choice for instruction.

Until the 1860s, sign language was the primary method used to educate deaf people.[6] Around that time, campaigns to replace sign language with lipreading and speech regained momentum and coincided with social and cultural changes occurring in the United States. A younger generation of educators was influenced by theories of evolution and argued that sign language was inferior to spoken language.[7] In 1867 the first private oral school opened in New York City.[8] Soon after, Alexander Graham Bell appeared in the United States and began holding exhibitions at the Boston School for Deaf Mutes in 1871.[9] As an opponent of sign language, Bell offered educators of deaf people another pedagogical option, "visible speech," which was "a system of universal alphabetics, originated by A. Melville Bell."[10] Bell's father "pioneered the use of 'visible speech,' a system he invented, which correlated all speech sounds with particular visual symbols as a way to assist deaf children to learn to speak."[11] Taking the method his father had devised,

Bell claimed he could teach deaf children how to perfectly position their mouths to produce clear sounds. Not surprisingly, Bell promoted oralism; he recommended that deaf students learn to speak and lipread rather than use sign language. Holding exhibitions, Bell asked deaf students to speak in front of audiences to demonstrate the successes of his oralist method. In reality, many of Bell's successful students were children who had become deaf postlingually, that is, after learning to speak, and had retained some of their speaking ability.[12] In spite of this issue, Bell's oral arguments and pedagogical methods made an impact on schools for deaf students in the United States in the late nineteenth and early twentieth centuries.

In 1891, the *American Annals of the Deaf* recorded a total of sixty-two public schools and fifteen private schools for deaf children in the United States, serving 9,232 deaf students. These schools subscribed to one of three teaching methods: oralism, manualism, or a combined method. Very few (if any) of these schools truly subscribed to manualism by this time. The *Annals* recorded that the majority of these *private* schools were oral schools; however, the majority of these *public* schools claimed to subscribe to a combined method of teaching. Ideally, the combined method took the best of the oral and manual methods to help all students to learn sign language and written English and to offer some of them training in speech and/or lipreading. However, many of the schools that claimed to subscribe to the combined method actually favored oralism and actually practiced little or no manualism, according to E. M. Gallaudet: "[I]t will be seen that the Combined System as it exists in America today includes schools where the pure oral method prevails."[13] True proponents of the combined method recognized that not all students benefited from learning speech or lipreading, but some of them, occasionally those who became deaf later in childhood, became skilled speakers and lipreaders with practice. While the combined method continued to make use of sign language in the classrooms for deaf students, strictly oral schools removed sign language altogether or relegated its use to religious training and chapel services.[14] Although this use of sign language may seem like a contradiction to the definition of a purely oral school, it is this specific use of sign language—for religious training—that problematizes the oral versus manual debates. On this point, E. M. Gallaudet found common ground with oralists: He argued that deaf students should continue to have religious training and chapel services in sign language regardless of the chosen method of instruction. Before examining his arguments for a combined method that emphasized sign language, let's explore the shift in deaf education that emerged in the mid-nineteenth century, which placed greater emphasis on speech and lipreading.

Oralism, Homogeneity, and Eugenics

In the United States, late nineteenth-century arguments opposing sign language and viewing deafness as a deficit were influenced by a desire for a national identity marked by spoken English, theories of evolution, and scientific thinking—stark contrasts to the manualists' earlier arguments grounded in Protestant theology. The deaf community in that era came under threat by oralists, who viewed the use of sign language as evidence that deaf individuals were excluded from American society. Schools for deaf Americans became sites where these arguments played out. Oral schools based their teaching methods on the goal of bringing deaf students into American society and helping them develop their intellect through the use of speech. For many who supported the oral method, speaking English was an important symbol of national unity.

After 1865, when the United States was recovering from the effects of the Civil War, Americans began to place emphasis on a unified identity. Oralism became a product of this national climate. Seeking homogeneity through language and culture, oralists argued that deaf Americans needed to learn to speak English in order to assimilate. It was partly this thinking and the influence of theories of evolution that bolstered the oralists' resolve.

It is no coincidence that oralists gained ground in the latter half of the nineteenth century, for it was in 1859 that Charles Darwin's *Origin of Species* was first published. Darwin's theory of natural selection provided an ideology for the oralists' arguments, whereas the manualists' contentions were often founded on a Protestant ideology. Baynton explains that fueling the oral movement in the late nineteenth century was an American culture that "thought in terms of scientific naturalism, especially evolutionary theory."[15] Darwin's theory was used to justify the oralists' view that sign language was inferior to speech. It was common thinking at that time that humans relied on sign language before they mastered speech.[16] Manualists interpreted this view in Protestant terms: Sign language was an original language, and its users were "closer to the Creation," not inferior.[17] However, oralists associated sign language with lower evolution or "inferior races."[18] They argued that deaf students needed to learn spoken English and lipreading; otherwise, they would be viewed as animals or savages. Contradicting the Protestant view of the manualists, post-Darwinian oralists of nineteenth-century America viewed sign language use in evolutionary terms:

> In an evolutionary age, language was no longer an inherent attribute of the human soul, one of an indivisible cluster of traits that included reason, imagination, and the conscience, conferred by God at the Creation. It was, instead, a distinct ability achieved through a process of evolution from animal ancestors. Sign language came to be seen as a language low on the scale of evolutionary progress, preceding in history even the most "savage" of spoken languages, and supposedly forming a link between the animal and the human.[19]

Considering sign language as a sign of a lower stage of evolution, oralists garnered support for the oral method of deaf education. Their claims appealed to the desire to bring deaf people "up" to a human level with the use of spoken English. Oralists gained support by using evolutionary theories to suggest that sign language was a primitive form of communication.

One of the strongest proponents of the oral method was Alexander Graham Bell, for whom speech reflected the value of being human.[20] Although he had a hard of hearing mother and a deaf wife, Bell wanted to see an end to sign language and deafness. Using his notoriety and wealth from inventing the telephone, Bell supported the oral method and the end of sign language.[21] His opposition to manualism served as the culmination of the oralists' argument—deafness threatened a national identity, evolutionary thinking showed sign language to be inferior to speech, and advancement in scientific thinking demonstrated that deafness indicated a deficit. Combining his interests in eugenics and deaf education, Bell argued that the nation would face a "great calamity" due to the high rate of intermarriage among deaf people.[22] After conducting his own investigation of the records of several American schools for deaf students, Bell presented his findings to a meeting of the American Academy of Sciences at New Haven, Connecticut, in 1883. Bell concluded from his study that intermarriages between congenitally deaf adults would result in "a deaf variety of the human race" that would be "a defective race of human beings."[23] His conclusion echoes both the concern for a unified national identity and the evolutionary lens that influenced his analysis. Bell perceived problems with creating a law that would prevent deaf individuals from marrying each other; he claimed the result would be sexual promiscuity and illegitimate children. Instead, he proposed preventive measures that included the elimination of residential schools, sign language use in schools for deaf children, and deaf teachers in deaf schools.[24] Bell wanted to dismantle the American deaf community that had emerged from the schools where manualism and Protestant ideology were intertwined.

While the deaf community had been viewed as a collective group early on in the nineteenth century, it was in Christian terms. Thomas H. Gallaudet's description of deaf Americans was that they were heathens, thus emphasizing the need for the salvation of an individual's soul. The oral method offered deaf Americans an opportunity to learn to speak and lipread, skills that oralists argued would allow them to interact and to participate in society at large. Historian Douglas C. Baynton thoroughly examines the context of the emergence of oralism in American schools for deaf children: "Oralists likened the deaf community to a community of immigrants" because "the use of sign language encouraged deaf people to associate principally with each other and to avoid the hard work of learning to communicate in spoken English."[25] The oralists offered a shift in thinking in the latter half of the nineteenth century that considered deaf Americans who used sign language as outsiders to the American culture, which was partially defined by spoken English. This argument was in line with anti-immigrant thinking in the latter half of the nineteenth century and the early twentieth century.

Manualism Supported by Protestant Practice and Theology

The change in national climate in late nineteenth-century America caused deaf community leaders to protect sign language use at the most fundamental levels—at the schools for deaf children. Carrying on his father's mission, Edward Miner Gallaudet entered the field of deaf education and became an advocate of sign language use and a leader in the American deaf community. In 1850, he became the first superintendent of the Columbia Institution for the Instruction of the Deaf and Dumb and the Blind, which was funded by Amos Kendall, a prominent Washington philanthropist. In 1864, President Abraham Lincoln signed a bill allowing the Columbia Institution to grant college degrees, and the school divided into two departments, the second of which was the National Deaf-Mute College. Edward M. Gallaudet is most widely recognized as the president of this first college in the United States for deaf students. In 1893 the name was changed again, this time to Gallaudet College in honor of Thomas Hopkins Gallaudet.[26] Since 1986, the school has been recognized as Gallaudet University. The long legacy of the Gallaudet family in deaf education in the United States is the preservation of the deaf community and sign language despite the efforts of oralists like Bell. Edward M. Gallaudet's opinions on deaf education were valued by the deaf community just as much as his father's were. And with changing pedagogical philosophies, Edward M. Gallaudet deviated slightly from his father's original teaching methods.

As Edward M. Gallaudet's experiences grew and his exposure to the oralists' teachings persisted, he began advocating a combined method that purported to best accommodate individual students' needs and abilities. He held that students who were capable of speech should be allowed the benefit of the oralists' techniques to improve their articulation. He warned, however, of the danger of enforcing this method of teaching on all students inasmuch as many would never learn a language at all if oralism were the only technique employed. He recognized that many deaf students would never be able to articulate speech and would best be served by instruction in sign language and written English. Edward Gallaudet argued that at the center of the combined method was deaf students' goal of becoming productive members of society and forming their own religious convictions.[27] The only way they could achieve these goals, according to Edward M. Gallaudet, was through the continuous use of sign language—even if it were in addition to oral practices.

The American deaf community faced oralists at home who found great support from their peers abroad. In the late nineteenth century, it was clear that manual practices were in the minority on an international front. Leaders in the education of deaf students met at the Milan Congress in 1880, an offshoot of the

International Congress for the Improvement of the Condition of Deaf-Mutes held two years earlier. Brothers Edward and Thomas Gallaudet Jr. were two of five U.S. representatives at the Milan Congress. Among the five U.S. delegates, James Denison, principal of Kendall School in Washington, DC, was the only deaf representative in attendance. At the conference, a motion was passed valuing speech over signs:

> The Convention, considering the incontestable superiority of speech over signs, (1) for restoring deaf-mutes to social life, and (2) for giving them greater facility of language, declares that the method of articulation should have the preference over that of signs in the instruction and education of the deaf and dumb.[28]

The delegates from the United States cast five of the six votes against the motion. Although the American deaf community was being attacked by proponents of oralism at home and abroad, its members were also becoming a community with leaders willing to fight for the preservation of sign language.

Edward Gallaudet frequently presented and published on the virtues of the combined method, citing the significance of sign language in the deaf community and the benefits of the oral method for some students. In a speech delivered to the Second Congress of the British Deaf and Dumb Association in Glasgow in August 1891 and published in the *American Annals of the Deaf* in October 1891, Edward Gallaudet echoes his father's use of religious themes, references, and reasoning to support his argument. He concludes his speech by quoting from scripture, specifically Mark 7:37: "It was said in proof of the divine beneficence of our Saviour's mission upon the earth: 'He hath done all things well, for he maketh the deaf to hear and the dumb to speak.' "[29]

Speaking in front of a large assembly of educators of deaf students in Great Britain and Ireland, Edward Gallaudet, like his father before him, acted as an ambassador for the American deaf community. It is also important to note the impetus for Edward

James Denison. (Gallaudet University Archives, Washington, DC)

Gallaudet's invitation to speak at the conference. In his biographical account of Gallaudet College he notes that

> I made the address on the combined system of educating the deaf before a large assemblage on the evening of August 7th. My invitation to address the Congress was suggested by Mrs. Francis Maginn of Belfast who was a student in our college a few years earlier and, at the time of my visit to Glasgow, a missionary to the deaf-mutes of Belfast and vicinity.[30]

Once again the intertwining of Protestant theology and deaf education is evident in this student who went on to become a missionary to other deaf people, continuing T. H. Gallaudet's work of saving the "deaf heathens." Edward Gallaudet's speech was published in both the *Annals* and the *Silent World,* where it reached an even wider audience. Readers of these periodicals were involved in the American deaf community and were thus particularly interested in the education of deaf children.

As mentioned earlier, Edward Gallaudet explored the benefits of both the manual and the oral methods of instruction, stressing that the manual method alone afforded more opportunities to deaf people both in education and religion than the oral method alone. He claimed that "by the practice of the manual method alone, with no aid from the oral, the entire body of the deaf can be so trained and educated as to become intelligent, happy, self-respecting, self-supporting, God-fearing members of society."[31] He also addressed the oralists' concerns that sign language would separate deaf individuals from a unified national identity. For Edward Gallaudet, the deaf students' religious beliefs and practices demonstrated their membership in an American society that still valued Protestant theology even with the advancement of evolutionary thinking. In addition, he wrote that "the gift to the deaf of the language of signs and the manual alphabet is of far greater value and comfort" than speech and lipreading.[32] Early manualists like T. H. Gallaudet referred to sign language as a gift that God gave deaf people. His son Edward also spoke of sign language in terms of a gift, as did many manualists of his time because, for them, sign language was a manifestation of divine providence. Weighing the benefits of signs against speech and lipreading, Edward Gallaudet continued to use religious references as his father had done several decades earlier.

For example, a central theme in Edward Gallaudet's argument for the combined method is the importance of the moral life of deaf students and the role that religious training plays in this. In support of his emphasis on manualism, he quotes oralists who claim that, without sign language, deaf students' moral states would be challenged. For Edward Gallaudet, then, part of the value of sign language is its significance in religious teaching and moral training. Appealing to the oralists in the audience, he cites the work of "a disciple of [Samuel] Heinicke, the founder of the oral method" and a name that would be familiar to the audience—Moritz Hill.[33] After a long career spent instructing deaf students in Germany, Hill compiled his reflections and views on the various methods used to teach deaf students. Edward Gallaudet quotes Hill in order to show the important advantages of the use of sign language, that is, the manual method. In this quotation, Hill, who was traditionally associated with the oral method, points out that it is important that sign language be used in the religious training of deaf students:

> [I]t is particularly in the teaching of religion that the language of pantomime plays an important part, especially when it is not only necessary to instruct, but to operate on sentiment and will, either because here this language is indispensable to express the moral state of man, his thoughts, and his actions, or that the word alone *makes too little impression on the eyes of the mute* to produce, without the aid of pantomime, the desired effect in a manner sure and sufficient.[34]

Hill recognizes that, in order to reach the souls of the deaf students in his care, sign language would have to be used because the spoken word is ineffective in religious teaching. His concession with regard to the effects of sign language compromises Hill's purely oralist standing. Hill expresses what many supporters of sign language maintained, that the true invocation of pathos for deaf individuals is through their natural language, sign language. Although Hill's explanation of the use of sign language in religious training is similar to Thomas Gallaudet's early nineteenth-century mission to teach sign language to deaf American students, Hill did not view sign language in the same way as manualists in the United States. To illustrate Hill's stance on sign language, Edward Gallaudet quotes Hill's more complete opinion of sign language:

> [I]t must be remembered that in his school, as in other oral schools where his views prevail, the language of signs is nothing more, to quote his own words, than "a very imperfect natural production, because it remains for the most part abandoned to a limited sphere of haphazard culture."[35]

Expressing disagreement with Hill on this latter view of sign language, Edward Gallaudet reminds his audience that sign language has been carefully developed for many generations. He also disagrees with Hill's claim that sign language is needed to teach deaf students religion and maintains that Hill's opinion of the use of sign language is similar to that of oralists who align deafness and sign language use with less evolved species like apes.[36] Edward Gallaudet presents evidence from oralists to demonstrate his thorough knowledge of the oral method and to indicate that he does not dismiss the oral method entirely. He appeals to them by citing a leading oralist whose teachings many oralists are familiar with. This strategy demonstrates his attempt to persuade pure oralists in the audience that it is in the best interest of all deaf students for religious training to be conducted in sign language, thus ensuring the preservation of sign language among deaf students at oral schools.

Like his father, Edward Gallaudet subscribed to a Protestant theology that placed a high priority on learning and teaching the gospels. If all educators of deaf students—whether manualists, oralists, or combinists—viewed sign language as the best method for teaching religion to deaf students, then the early manualists' arguments that sign language was a gift from God would be sustained. Early manualists were Protestants who believed that sign language was "a language closer to God and nature than speech, uncorrupted and pure, more honest because more direct as a means of emotional expression."[37] For Edward Gallaudet, sign language was quite useful in religious services in order to convey "clear, vivid, and often eloquent expression, incomparably superior to anything the pure oral method can furnish."[38] For him, sign language provided deaf Americans with a natural and easy means of communicating. As mentioned earlier, sign language was referred to as "a gift to the deaf" and intertwined with religious references by Edward Gallaudet throughout "The Combined Systems of Instruction." This view of sign language epitomized his view of education, which was more than simply preparing for a vocation. Based on his alignment of sign language with morality, religious training, and even salvation, Edward Gallaudet's perception of education included a higher cause: the shaping of students' character. If pure oral schools were to persist, deaf students would not learn sign language and, as a result, would have neither a strong grasp of practical knowledge nor a foundation in religious teachings. In addition, purely oral schools would produce deaf individuals who would be unable to participate in either American society at large or a deaf community. He claimed that "[t]he most serious criticism which may justly be brought against the *pure* oral method is that it *cannot* be successfully applied to all the deaf."[39] As mentioned earlier, not all deaf students are capable of speaking and lipreading. These are skills that come easier to some than to others. For this reason, Edward Gallaudet opposed pure oralism but saw value in it when it was combined with manualism.

Maintaining that the best elements of both oralism and manualism could be combined, Edward Gallaudet argued, in "The Combined System of Instruction," for pure oral schools (of which there were many in the late nineteenth century) to include the use of sign language. However, his article was just as much for pure manualists as it was for pure oralists. Persuaded by his counterparts in Europe and cases in the United States, he acknowledged that those deaf students who were capable of learning speech in fact benefited from doing so. At the core of the combined system, he claimed, was the desire to provide an education that best met the needs and capabilities of the individual student. The use of both methods, he asserted, would demonstrate that educators of deaf children were following the example of Christ in the gospels. Edward Gallaudet concluded his thoughts by reflecting on the service of educating deaf children in Protestant religious terms:

> Following his benign examples, let us in his spirit go forward in the work we have to do, striving with singleness of purpose, and with every means coming to our hands, so to train those whom "the finger of God hath touched" that they may at length, with ears indeed unstopped, hear the welcome, "Well done, good and faithful servant," and with tongues made musical for the melody of Heaven join in the harmonies of the life that knows no imperfection and no end.[40]

Like his father, Edward Gallaudet emphasized that it was imperative to teach deaf people in sign language so that they, too, could know God. At the heart of this idea was also his concern for their religious state (salvation, in Protestant terms). In Protestant theology, in order for deaf people to experience their ears becoming "unstopped" and to be able to anticipate life in Heaven, they would need to know God and repent of their sins. According to Edward Gallaudet's emotional and ethical appeal, to deny the deaf students sign language would be analogous to denying them entrance to Heaven and the miracle of hearing and speaking.

Like Edward Gallaudet, other educators also expressed their own concern for the religious training of deaf students. For example, in 1892 the Reverend Philip J. Hasenstab argued for all teachers of deaf students to be knowledgeable about religion in order to foster the students' spiritual development: "It is not sufficient merely to teach a child to read and write, but he must be educated, *i.e.*, led forth out of the darkness into light. . . . This means to secure him the blessing of becoming an intelligent human creature in all possible ways, physical, mental, moral, and

Philip J. Hasenstab. (Gallaudet University Archives, Washington, DC)

spiritual."[41] Hasenstab argued that it is the instructor's duty to teach students the "truth as taught in the Bible."[42] He thus represented the views of many deaf educators who were also ministers. His personal religious beliefs, like those of Thomas and Edward Gallaudet, influenced his particular emphasis in deaf education: religious training. Hasenstab wanted to ensure that deaf students would know right from wrong and become followers of Christ's teachings. As an advocate of the combined system, Hasenstab insisted that instructors use whatever method was necessary for deaf students to receive religious training: "By all means find some proper channel through which to pour new ideas into his soul. He should be so prepared that he will minister as well as be ministered to."[43] The spiritual state of the deaf students was so important to him that he supported whatever method—oral or manual—would help them learn the gospels and become practitioners of them. Like Edward Gallaudet, Hasenstab advocated religious training for deaf students; however, unlike Hasenstab, Edward Gallaudet supported sign language as the most sufficient conveyor of religious training for all deaf students.

To show how ingrained this idea of sign language use is to the saving of deaf souls as expressed by Edward Gallaudet in the conclusion of "The Combined System of Instruction," I offer a look back at snapshots from the American School for the Deaf reunion in 1850. More than two hundred former students gathered on September 26, 1850, to recognize and celebrate the work of Laurent Clerc and T. H. Gallaudet to teach sign language to deaf students in the United States. In expressing their gratitude, the former students and their teachers stood up and signed their appreciation for the efforts of these men in teaching them about the gospels:

> Thirty-three years ago, the deaf mutes in this country were in darkness of the grossest ignorance. They knew not God. They knew nothing of the maker of heaven and earth. They knew nothing of the mission of Jesus Christ into the world to pardon sin. They knew not that, after this life, God would reward the virtuous and punish the vicious. They knew no distinction between right and wrong. They were all in ignorance and poverty, with no means of conveying their ideas to others, waiting for instruction, as the sick for a physician to heal them.[44]

Attributing the manual instruction that Clerc and T. H. Gallaudet brought to those deaf students in the Hartford area with the aim of saving of their souls, alumni in their presentations at the reunion overwhelmingly mentioned the instruction of and in sign language with their journeys from "darkness" to "light." In his remarks to T. H. Gallaudet, former student and teacher George H. Loring signed the following:

> It is fortunate and it was also by a kind dispensation of Divine Providence, that you adopted the best method of instruction of the deaf and dumb. By this method we have been instructed in the principles of language, morality and religion, and this education has qualified us to be useful members of society.[45]

Citing many of the manualists' arguments, Loring acknowledged that the use of sign language in the schools was a key element of the deaf students' religious training. At the same time he expressed a common manual viewpoint that sign language use and advocacy are intertwined with the Protestant perspective that sign language is a gift from God.

Many years later, Edward Gallaudet would argue that looking back at the first permanent school for deaf children, which his father led and so many of the alumni at the 1850 reunion admired, was a good starting point for determining the necessary criteria for a model school for deaf students. In 1892 he repeated many of his earlier arguments for the combined system of instruction and continued to emphasize the importance of education. Listing what the Hartford School had done right, Edward Gallaudet mentioned the "careful undenominational training in religion, with interesting Sabbath services."[46] He also acknowledged that the Hartford School's success was evident in its continued service to deaf students. It had helped to educate many deaf Americans and preserve sign language in difficult times and maintained religious training as part of its curriculum.

Edward Gallaudet also indicated what he believed was necessary for a model school for deaf children in the late nineteenth century. Three of the twelve items he listed include references to religion. He argued that the school's leader should have religious convictions and be "prepared to inspire and develop veneration for God and the highest moral aims."[47] He also stated that, in a true combined system, students who are taught orally should have the benefit of religious services in sign language.[48] In addition, he reiterated the importance of religious teachings in this model school:

> Religious instruction of an undenominational character should occupy a prominent and honored place, and this instruction should be given in the language through which alone the mind and heart of the deaf can be moved and impressed as the mind and heart of the hearing are through audible speech.[49]

Edward Gallaudet's argument for a model school for deaf children continued to link sign language use to religious teaching and training. Specifically, sign language advocacy by manualists reflected the worldview they imparted to the deaf students in their schools. Even though Edward Gallaudet makes references to nondenominational religious instruction, the God he hoped deaf students would come to fear was a personal God based on Protestant theology.

Epistemology and Deaf Education: *Arizona Cactus*

As we have already seen, oralists and manualists differed ideologically with regard to deaf education. In late nineteenth-century arguments for oralism, speech was indicative of intellect. According to the oralists, deaf students exhibited a halted intellect or even a lack of intellect if they were unable to speak. Despite the oralists' grounding in new scientific thinking, deaf individuals were prospering as a result of their educations at manual and combined-method schools. One reason for this was the training they received in a trade while there. These vocational classes grew in number after the Civil War, as many schools began emphasizing industrial education and expanding the number of trades they taught.[50] At the turn of the century, more focused vocational training enabled deaf students to learn how to use the printing presses that were turning out school publications. These publications often reflected the continued connection between the American deaf community and Protestant theology even after an increase in nonsectarian and secularist practices in education. To illustrate this, I examine one such publication titled the

Arizona Cactus, from the Arizona School for the Deaf and Blind (ASDB).

The ASDB opened in 1912 in Tucson. Initially this state school was a department of the University of Arizona, and its first location was a converted residence on campus.[51] The major artifact of the ASDB is its quarterly publication, the *Arizona Cactus*. In 1918 the ASDB moved to fifty acres donated by the City of Tucson and purchased eighteen additional acres before the *Arizona Cactus* was first published in 1926. The publication served many purposes. Vocationally, it gave students experience in printing and training in the trade. It also served as a newsletter with announcements for school faculty and parents who sent their children to live at the residential school. Often included in each issue were serialized historical pieces and works by students. Significantly for this study is the fact that these publications frequently included poems or writings that contained religious references and themes. Before examining the examples from the *Arizona Cactus*, I provide some historical context to better illustrate the significance of ASDB's religious writings in a time of more secularization in public education.

The first shift away from specific religious-focused instruction in schools was to nondenominational teachings, which often focused on Protestant theology as opposed to Catholic. Specific denominational tracts or teachings were forbidden at state schools at the turn of the century. In 1918 Stephen Beauregard Weeks cited an 1879 law that declared that state schools should not reflect any denominational qualities:

> Another section of this law—an echo of the struggle in 1877 against the proposed union of the church and state—was the thirty-eighth, which declares:
>
> "No books, tracts, or papers of a sectarian or denominational character shall be used or introduced in any school established under the provisions of this act; nor shall sectarian or denominational doctrine be taught therein; nor shall any school whatever receive any of the public school funds which has not been taught in accordance with provisions of this act."[52]

The ASDB was established after the law of 1879 was enacted and thus was subject to the law, which denied state support to any school whose publications contained religious references pertinent to a specific denominational persuasion. And after Arizona was admitted to the Union on February 14, 1912, federal grants awarded one hundred thousand acres "for schools and asylums for the deaf, dumb, and the blind," further solidifying the relationship between ASDB and the state.[53] To stress the separation of church and state, Weeks stated the following:

> The new constitution provided that no sectarian instruction should ever be imparted in any school or state educational institution, and that no religious or political test of qualifications should be required as condition of admission to any public educational institution as teacher, student, or pupil.[54]

Although we have no indication that ASDB tested students on religious matters, certain evidence suggests that Protestant theology found a niche in the moral teachings, which still held a primary spot in residential schools for deaf children. Even though specific denominational teachings may not have been presented, ASDB, like other state-funded schools for deaf students, provided religious training that was Protestant and thus emphasized that students may have personal relationships with God.

Even though Weeks clearly states that the laws called for secularization in education, he uses Protestant rhetoric to explain the leadership in Arizona that changed education for the better. Describing Governor Safford, Weeks writes, "The new governor appeared in 1869. He was Anson P. K. Safford, and from California came this new Moses, destined to lead Arizona from darkness to educational light."[55] Echoing the manualists' frequent metaphor about sign language bringing deaf students out of the darkness of ignorance and into the light of reason and knowledge of God, Weeks likens Safford to Moses, who led the Israelites out of the desert and into a closer relationship with God. For Weeks, Safford's development of the Arizona schools and the organization he applied to the public school system was equally important.

Weeks's use of this religious metaphor suggests that, despite the aforementioned Arizona law calling for separation between overt denominational theology and education in state-supported schools like ASDB, such statutes may not have been in widespread practice until much later in the twentieth century. As Ignatius Bjorlee points out,

> The first schools of our land were religious schools. Pupils were taught to read in order that they might know the Bible. The divergent nature of our religious beliefs has made the pursuance of such course in our public schools impossible, hence the non sectarian. Moral and ethical principles are universal and through precept and example the way is paved and encouragement lent toward denominational teachings in accordance with the dictates of conscience and the word of God, as variously interpreted.[56]

Although nonsectarian and nondenominational teaching was stressed, Bjorlee points out that ties to Protestant theology and ethical principles closely linked to personal relationships with God still found their way into the state schools for deaf children via moral training.

As evidence of the Protestant footprints in U.S. schools for deaf students, religious references were often found in school writings relevant to deaf lives, even at a state-funded school like ASDB. Protestant themes that emerged in the religious pieces in the *Arizona Cactus* focused on morality, the comfort of being a creation of God, and coming to knowledge through a relationship with God. Like the arguments of manualists in the nineteenth century, the religious references in the early twentieth-century ASDB publications indicate a connection between knowledge and Protestant theology. Howard Griffin reflects on what schools should inculcate in their students:

> Regard for the rights of others, adaptation to the environment in which he must live, order and discipline, simple rules of ethics, fundamental principals [*sic*] of religion, all these and more are lived daily, and these together with what comes through the mastery of English and a few allied subjects, the child is pretty well balanced.[57]

Griffin goes on to claim that a background in religion is important for a student to "go forward in life."[58] For many educators in American schools for the deaf, teachings in morality were often synonymous with religious training. Even though some state schools may have practiced nondenominational religious teaching, the ASDB's *Arizona Cactus* indicates that belief in a God that could transcend worldly troubles and sorrows was at the core of the institution's worldview.

Encouraging moral living and a belief in God, the *Arizona Cactus* published poems with strong Protestant themes. Its first issue offered readers the poem "Just This Minute," which states, "Just this minute we are going / Toward right or toward wrong; / Just this minute we are sowing / Seeds of sorrow or of song. / Just this minute we are thinking / On the ways that lead to God, / Or in idle dreams are sinking / To the level of the clod."[59] The poem stresses the importance of living a moral life, and in this poem, "moral" is equivalent to thoughts and actions that reflect Christian beliefs. The poem also alludes to what Protestant followers would find familiar: Galatians 6:7. Generally associated with sowing and reaping, the verse reads, "Be not deceived; God is not mocked: for whatsoever a man soweth, that shall he also reap." The sentiment of the verse is echoed in the poem. In Protestant theology, serving God with thoughts and actions that are pleasing would bring rewards in Heaven. By featuring such a poem in the school publication, the ASDB demonstrates a religious influence intertwined with deaf education, one that encouraged deaf students to come to know God personally.

Another theme that emerges in the *Arizona Cactus* is the comfort that deaf students could find in knowing they were created by God, which is exemplified in the poem "God Made Them All." Demonstrating the belief that all things come from God, the poem states, "All things bright and beautiful, / All creatures great and small, / All things wise and wonderful, / The Lord God made them all."[60] Students who attended the ASDB lived away from their parents and hearing siblings. Although many stories testify to the comfort deaf students found in coming together and meeting other deaf people at deaf schools, they were frequently reminded that they were unlike hearing people. A poem such as "God Made Them All" reminded the students and students' families that they were alike in that they shared the same creator—God. For some students, this Protestant belief may have brought comfort; for manualists, it reinforced the belief that deaf students were not only capable of learning but also worthy of religious teaching so they could come to know God.

In contrast, the *Tucsonian*, initially a weekly publication that later became the annual of Tucson High School, has very few, if any, references to religious teaching or religious practices among the students. Tucson High School was and still is a peer institution of ASDB. Just a few miles southeast of ASDB, it historically served hearing students in the Tucson area. Students worked with faculty to publish the *Tucsonian*, which the June 1908 issue states is "devoted to high school interests." The *Tucsonian* served as the school paper for at least the first ten years of its existence, and in 1920 it became a traditional high school yearbook—with less and less writing and more and more pictures of students. Included in each issue of the earlier weekly periodical are "editorials; a joke department and local items; interscholastic sports are discussed; amusing and entertaining stories are given considerable space, and much advertising matter is printed, just as in a newspaper."[61] Articles in the early editions of the *Tucsonian* are not unlike items found in school papers of today; however, the *Tucsonian* provides a stark contrast to ASDB's *Arizona Cactus*. Instead of including poems that reflected on Protestant beliefs, editors of the

Tucsonian published poems that contemplated the surrounding desert landscape, such as "The Lone Outlaw" and "The Desert." Leah Hamilton, the Tucson High School sophomore who wrote both poems, describes the "lonely desert's treeless plain" as "long lines of burning, barren, glittering sand."[62] Other poems such as "To the Sun," "The Coming of Autumn," and "Westward Ho" reflect students' experiences of life in the Southwest. What is more, none of these poems has any biblical or Protestant religious references, unlike those in the *Arizona Cactus*.

Protestant references surfaced throughout the early editions of the *Arizona Cactus*. Seasonal greetings often included quotes of Bible verses, and one historical piece recounting the role of deaf people in history starts with the story of Jesus performing a miracle: "One day while Jesus was preaching to a crowd of people on the shore of Galilee, some one [*sic*] brought to Him a man who was a deaf-mute. Jesus [felt] sorry for him and said: 'Ephphatha' and his ear[s] were opened and he could speak again."[63] This story from Mark 7:32–35 is often cited in deaf narratives. Many members of the deaf community of the day often associated the command "be opened" (*ephphatha*) with the minds of deaf people, thus the need to utilize the best method of education. This selection is also a reminder that deaf students were responsible for printing the *Arizona Cactus*. Although the quote contains some errors, it is possible that they were in the original manuscript submitted by the author, who is not acknowledged but in all likelihood was a student.

"The Deaf in History" is a short article that recounts part of Jesus's life, beginning with the healing of the deaf man, and later mentions the opening of a college for deaf students in the late nineteenth century. It ends in 1936, which would have been the current time for the author, a period when many such schools had opened all over the world.[64] It is a familiar account of the history of deaf people in the United States because the author cites the influence of T. H. Gallaudet on deaf education. Evident in this article are the influence of religious teachings in schools for deaf students and the story of T. H. Gallaudet as the father of deaf education in the United States. "The Deaf in History" demonstrates the ability of deaf students to acquire knowledge and to use written English while attending a school that values the use of sign language among deaf students.

Conclusion

The teaching methods advocated by Edward Gallaudet and Bell at the end of the nineteenth century had lasting impacts on the deaf community. Today, many have adapted Bell's arguments to pursue scientific means to eliminate deafness. We see this with the advancement of technology and cochlear implants and with genetic testing to isolate the hereditary cause of hearing loss. This view of deafness as a deficit is contrasted by deaf community members who cite deaf people's productivity in society and life in general as evidence they are not lacking. Edward Gallaudet would not completely agree with this current viewpoint in the deaf community; however, he did support the use of sign language, especially to train deaf students in religion. For Edward Gallaudet, nondenominational religious training favoring Protestantism was important for the American schools for the deaf to maintain, and he argued that this training needed to be conducted in sign language. What emerged from this practice was the site of the sanctuary in advocacy for sign language. Because many oralists and manualists agreed that chapel services in the schools for the deaf should be conducted in sign language for all students, sign language persevered. This meant that the sanctuary became a location where, despite oralists' motives to eliminate sign language, it flourished and was transmitted throughout the American deaf community.

Notes

1. *Combinists* subscribed to and employed the "combined method," which utilized both manual and oral instruction. By the latter part of the nineteenth century, educators of deaf students who were formally pure manualists offered those students who would benefit from it instruction in speech and speechreading.

2. Van Cleve and Crouch, *Place of Their Own,* 112.

3. Weld, "American Asylum," 107.

4. Ibid.

5. Ibid., 108.

6. See Baynton, "'Savages and Deaf-Mutes,'" 93; Van Cleve and Crouch, *Place of Their Own,* 106–27; Jankowski, *Deaf Empowerment,* 22.

7. Baynton, "'Savages and Deaf-Mutes,'" 93.

8. Krentz, *Mighty Change,* 112; Van Cleve and Crouch, *Place of Their Own,* 112.

9. Van Cleve and Crouch, *Place of Their Own,* 114.

10. Jenkins, "Professor A. Graham Bell's Studies on the Deaf," 117.

11. Greenwald, "Taking Stock," 137.

12. Van Cleve and Crouch, *Place of Their Own,* 115.

13. Edward Miner Gallaudet, "Combined System," 257.

14. The role of the sanctuary (e.g., chapel services at residential schools for deaf students in the United States) in sustaining and advocating sign language is the subject of the following chapter.

15. Baynton, *Forbidden Signs*, 9.

16. See Baynton, "'Savages and Deaf-Mutes,'" 98; Armstrong, *Original Signs*, 16–18; Stokoe, *Language in Hand*, 55.

17. Baynton, "'Savages and Deaf-Mutes,'" 98.

18. Baynton, *Forbidden Signs*, 9.

19. Baynton, "'Savages and Deaf-Mutes,'" 98.

20. Baynton, *Forbidden Signs*, 55.

21. Van Cleve and Crouch, *Place of Their Own*, 117.

22. Baynton, *Forbidden Signs*, 30.

23. Quoted in Van Cleve and Crouch, *Place of Their Own*, 146.

24. Ibid., 147.

25. Baynton, *Forbidden Signs*, 16.

26. Gallaudet, *History of the College*, 188.

27. Ibid., "Ideal School," 282.

28. Quoted in Van Cleve and Crouch, Place of Their Own, 110.

29. Gallaudet, "Combined System," 266.

30. Gallaudet, *History of the College*, 184.

31. Gallaudet, "Combined System," 259.

32. Ibid.
33. Ibid.
34. Quoted in ibid., 260. Emphasis in original.
35. Ibid.
36. See Baynton, "'Savages and Deaf-Mutes'"; Gallaudet, "Combined System," 261.
37. Baynton, *Forbidden Signs*, 9.
38. Gallaudet, "Combined System," 264.
39. Ibid., 261. Emphasis in original.
40. Ibid., 266.
41. Hasenstab, "Religious Training," 15–16.
42. Ibid., 18.
43. Ibid., 21.
44. Spofford, "Fisher Ames Spofford's Address," 143.
45. Loring, "George H. Loring's Address to Gallaudet," 147.
46. Gallaudet, "Ideal School for the Deaf," 282.
47. Ibid., 284.
48. Ibid., 285.
49. Ibid.
50. Baynton, *Forbidden Signs*, 97.
51. Averitt, *ASDB 75th Commemoration*, 2.
52. Weeks, *History of Public Education in Arizona*, 38.
53. Ibid., 88.
54. Ibid., 89.
55. Ibid., 130.
56. Bjorlee, "What Does Education Mean to You?" 21.
57. Howard Griffin, "What Shall We Teach?" 7.
58. Ibid.
59. "Just This Minute," 7.
60. "God Made Them All," 4.
61. "Why Do We have a High School Paper?" 1.
62. Hamilton, "Desert," 5; "Lone Outlaw," 30.
63. Valentine, "Deaf in History," 13.
64. Ibid.

3

Saved by Signs: The Role of the Sanctuary in the Preservation of Sign Language

Deaf rhetoric that asserted the divine root of sign language thereby claimed for it divine sanction.

—Susan Burch, *Signs of Resistance: American Deaf Cultural History, 1900–1942*

O master of all languages, we thank Thee for the power and the glory of the sign language . . . . Thou knowest what is best for the deaf, Thou art just.

—Arthur G. Leisman, "Prayers of the Deaf"

PROTESTANT chapel and church services were important factors in the preservation of sign language. Ministers and many deaf educators of the nineteenth and twentieth centuries argued for the practical use of sign language in the chapel at residential schools for deaf students. They believed that sign language was more effective than spoken language in reaching these students; thus sign language was the preferred method of delivering religious rhetoric. As students graduated and left the residential schools, it became important for them to continue interacting socially with other deaf individuals. The church offered this opportunity to the deaf community. Protestant churches became a sanctuary for sign language and the deaf community.

As the previous chapters show, education for deaf students in the United States began with a Protestant Christian influence. Thomas Hopkins Gallaudet, as a Congregationalist minister, maintained a curriculum at the first permanent school for deaf students in the United States and provided religious training and chapel services conducted in sign language. Once students completed their education at residential schools, they often found the church playing a significant role in their lives. Some Protestant churches continued the work of the residential school chapels by offering services in sign language for deaf adults, while others were made up of only deaf congregations. The first deaf church was St. Ann's Church for the Deaf-Mutes, which held its first Sunday services in October 1852. The Reverend Thomas Gallaudet Jr., the eldest son of T. H. Gallaudet, was the head minister at St. Ann's. Although he was trained like his brother, E. M. Gallaudet, in education, he went on to become an Episcopal minister. Gallaudet Jr. ministered to deaf people in the eastern part of the United States by delivering sermons in sign language and providing social opportunities and classes for deaf adults in the community. His work in ministering to deaf Americans is an example of how the sanctuary became a location where literal and symbolic arguments to protect sign language appeared.

These religious services also served the American deaf community as a social forum. As students went on to graduate and leave the residential schools throughout the late nineteenth and early twentieth centuries, they often found themselves in communities with very few other deaf individuals. In order to socialize with other adult deaf Americans, they began attending weekly worship services at hearing churches that provided interpreted services or one of the few churches for deaf people.

In this chapter I examine the importance of the church and the role of deaf school chapels in preserving sign language throughout the late nineteenth and twentieth centuries. I argue that because sign language was maintained in the church sanctuaries, sign language use and religious instruction are intertwined in the history of the American deaf community. I show that sign language flourished in the church and stabilized an emerging deaf community even well into the twentieth century. I demonstrate that ministers' religious rhetoric was effective only when delivered in sign language. The chapel services and Protestant churches attended by deaf students and deaf community members thus suggest a value system that was grounded in Protestant theology during the late nineteenth and twentieth centuries.

Following the Call: Late Nineteenth-Century Sanctuaries for Sign Language

From the inception of deaf education in the United States in 1817, religious instruction was an important component. As debates over teaching methods consumed the last half of the nineteenth century, the chapel was for the most part maintained as a signing place. Arguments even among advocates for oralism supported the use of sign language in religious instruction and chapel services (see chapter 2). For most of the ministers who used sign language in residential school chapels, arguments supporting their choice of communication were twofold. The first was practical: Sign language was appropriate because it was easier to see signs made by a minister in a pulpit than to read the minister's lips. The second reason had to do with the interpretive power of sign language. Many educators of and ministers to deaf students argued that sign language had the capability of conveying the abstract religious ideas that they were teaching deaf students better than spoken English. While the latter reasoning is closely related to the arguments of early nineteenth-century manualists, who considered it to be a language closer to God, it was also significant for the continued use of sign language in the chapel and eventually in the sanctuary.

As more schools for deaf students opened in the United States, the chapel emerged as a common facet in their lives despite school leaders' arguments about manualism, oralism, and the combined system, which aligned with opposing ideologies. Since many deaf schools were also residential schools, these institutions undertook not only scholastic training of students but also spiritual instruction. Attendance at religious services in chapels housed on the schools' property formed part of the students' school experience.

At these early schools, students spent a fair amount of time in religious services and religious instruction classes, more so than deaf students of the twentieth century. Historians Otto B. Berg and Henry L. Buzzard claim that the American School for the Deaf "became, in effect, a church, for the students were required to attend daily chapel exercises, they learned common Old Testament stories, were expected to be familiar with the parables, miracles, and principal events in the life of Christ as set down in the New Testament."[1] Thomas H. Gallaudet approached the education of deaf students in the United States as his mission work—to lead the unsaved deaf people to Christ. This significant starting point of deaf education continued to find its way into the curriculum or the social function of residential schools many decades after the first permanent American school opened in 1817.

The pivotal start of mission work to deaf people by Protestant churches began in the mid-nineteenth century. After teaching for six years in the New York School for the Deaf, Thomas Gallaudet Jr. decided to organize a Bible class for deaf adults in New York City. He was ordained in the Episcopal Church and became a priest in 1851. The Reverend Alexander MacLeod Manson claims that Thomas Gallaudet Jr.'s denominational choice for ministry was specific to the needs of deaf people, which he claimed the church could meet: Thomas Gallaudet Jr. "believed that [the Episcopal Church] embodied a form of worship which best suited the peculiar need in the ministry to the deaf."[2] The Episcopal Church organization would be able to fund a ministry for deaf people in New York and support Gallaudet's vision of a church for them.

Although Protestant churches offered ministries to deaf people, similar Episcopal ministries have been recognized as the most visible and the most active. In the nineteenth century, "religion work among the deaf was assumed initially by a remarkable succession of Episcopal clergymen."[3] Thomas Gallaudet Jr.'s plan for his ministry to deaf persons was to serve them through sign language and to provide them with a place that would become independently theirs. His plan stipulated the following:

1. The church was to adhere to the standards of the Protestant Episcopal Church.
2. It was to be kept free of debt.
3. It was to have a parish house in which there would be provisions for a reading room and free lecture courses.
4. The language of signs was to be the official language.
5. There was to be an assistant minister, so that the rector could be free to establish missions in other cities.
6. The church was to sponsor a home for the disabled and the superannuated deaf.
7. The church was to be self-supporting.[4]

After a few years of Bible classes and signed sermons offered at other sanctuaries, the first services at St. Ann's Church for Deaf-Mutes were held on October 2, 1852, in the chapel of New York University. In 1858 Thomas Gallaudet Jr. resigned from the New York School for the Deaf and entered full-time ministry at St. Ann's.

Thomas Gallaudet Jr. spent the rest of his life in full-time ministry serving the religious interests of deaf Americans of all races. Through his leadership, Thomas Gallaudet Jr. organized All Souls' in Philadelphia as a mission for deaf persons in 1859. All Souls' was later consecrated as a church for deaf people in 1888. During the next decade, nine other churches were erected as the work of the Episcopal mission to deaf individuals. These Protestant churches, like St. Ann's, took over the role of chapel services in the lives of deaf adults.

Transitions into a New Century

From its inception, St. Ann's Church also served as an advocate for the deaf community, as did many other Protestant churches.

As early as 1880, the Conference of Church Workers among the Deaf coordinated, promoted, and publicized the Episcopal Church's work for deaf people. These Episcopalian clergy and lay-workers who ministered to the deaf community met every three years, according to Manson. The Church Workers among the Deaf served as advocates for the American deaf community and stated their objectives as follows:

> To preach the Gospel of Jesus Christ to the Deaf.
> To promote the training of men for the work of ministering to the Deaf.
> To organize and advance the work in the new missionary fields.
> To join workers for the deaf in a common fellowship for the cause of Christ.
> To promote publicity and disseminate information about the missions to the deaf.
> To advance the Deaf in all matters religious, educational and social, to their benefit as a class.
> To establish an endowment fund for the stabilization and extension of the missionary work of the Protestant Episcopal Church among the Deaf in the United States.[5]

In advocating for deaf people in the United States, the Church Workers among the Deaf published letters in their magazine, *The Deaf Churchman*, addressing their objectives.

Because the churches for deaf people provided services in sign language, they were advocating its use and creating a site where it would continue to be used, thereby ensuring its preservation. The sanctuary that the Protestant churches provided deaf adults in late nineteenth- and early twentieth-century America by ministering to them in sign language was a significant factor in the stabilization of an emerging deaf community as recognized by its use of sign language.

In addition, the religious training of deaf students weighed heavily on older deaf community members who argued for the continued use of sign language in chapels at the turn of the twentieth century. In the June 1898 issue of the *Silent Worker*, the publication of the New Jersey School for the Deaf, one writer claims that only sign language can touch the hearts of deaf people: "[Y]ou will find but one way in which their hearts may be touched, their souls stirred, and the great truths of the Christian religion brought home to them . . . not through soundless mouthing, not always through the printed page, are the spirits of these people stirred."[6] The writer argues that the deaf congregant or student will be moved only by a sermon delivered in sign language by a master signer. It is the gracefulness of the signs, the writer contends, that appeals to the soul of the deaf congregant or student in a way that spoken English cannot. The writer states that when a deaf person is taken to

> a Church where the same Gospel truths are presented in the distinct and graceful gestures of the sign-language . . . [one may b]ehold how his eyes lighten, he is moved, he weeps, he prays. God speaks to him. It is music—the poetry of motion—a truly enlivening presentation of ideas. Spiritual force comes, kindling and enriching, through a happy medium that is to him what an eloquent voice or inspiring music is to his hearing brother.[7]

Like other members of the deaf community, this writer suggests that sign language was the only means to convey abstract religious theology to the deaf and the only medium that would lead to the conviction of the deaf.

Ministering to Deaf People: Twentieth-Century Sanctuaries

Nineteenth-century school practices, including religious training, are somewhat different from twentieth-century practices. Clint C. Sexton points out that "[t]he early schools for the deaf were headed by ministers and other people with strong religious beliefs. In fact, the Bible was included as one of their important textbooks. The pupils of those days spent longer hours in religious instruction than do the pupils in the residential schools today."[8] Sexton acknowledges that religious training was still occurring in state schools in the mid-twentieth century, when he was writing. While students in twentieth-century residential schools did not spend as many hours in religious training, chapel services were still in existence, and the chapel still functioned as a signing place.

Chapel services at twentieth-century residential schools maintained the role of linking religious teaching and sign language use. Like the earlier schools in the nineteenth century, twentieth-century schools offered sermons delivered in sign language. Ministers continued to argue that sign language was necessary in the chapel for students to effectively follow the sermon. Joseph Schuyler Long, a twentieth-century principal at the Iowa School for the Deaf and a Gallaudet College graduate, recognized "the very great value of signs . . . and its [*sic*] necessity in the pulpit and on the platform."[9] He claimed that, "in spiritual matters, signs enable the minister to reach thousands where any other method of communication would reach the few."[10] Long pointed out the obvious, that in the chapel signs are more effective than oral methods. It was much easier to read signs from pews several rows back from the pulpit than to read the minister's lips. Long also alluded to the power of sign language to reach the conscience of the deaf student in a way that spoken English cannot. He published the first edition of his text in 1909, a time when oralism was taking over as the chosen method of instruction in schools for deaf students. Because deaf leaders in education, like Long, continued to argue for its practical use in the chapel, sign language was maintained as a feature at predominantly oral schools, combined-system schools, and of course manual schools.

While the practicality of using sign language in the pulpit to address a fairly large deaf audience seems obvious, it was not the method practiced by every minister at every school. In the May

1900 issue of *The Silent Worker,* one writer proposes a solution to the problem of whether to deliver a sermon in signs or orally. The writer suggests using a large slate to "write out much of a lecture occupying twenty minutes or a half hour, and this supplemented by a little manual spelling and a trifle of 'acting out' may be a solution of the chapel question."[11] Manual spelling is not a signed language; it is using fingerspelling to spell words one letter at a time. This suggestion assumes that schools would have slate boards large enough to write an entire sermon on and that students would be able to read the words and follow along from several pews back. The writer claims that a hundred square feet of slate board space might be needed to write out a twenty-minute sermon. Another problem with this suggestion is the effect that a written sermon would have on the congregation's emotions.

Part of a minister's strength is the ability to connect with the congregation on some level and evoke a response. A written sermon for deaf students to read in a chapel setting while the minister delivers the message in English changes the rhetorical situation and in essence makes the sermon ineffective and fails to fulfill the minister's purpose. In this situation, the minister has removed the imperative rhetorical element of delivery, which is extremely important in addressing a deaf audience, whose first language is visual. Rhetorician and ethnographer Roxanne Mountford recognizes the importance of delivery in an oral setting: "An analysis of oral performance must begin with a recognition that the body is not only an instrument of expression but is also itself expressive of meaning."[12] In sign language, the body is instrumental in conveying meaning. Facial expressions and body positions are part of the delivery of signs. They not only provide emphasis and are the equivalent of intonation in oral performances but also carry elements of grammar that clarify the signer's message. Signs can also be exaggerated, made larger or smaller, to convey a particular point. One effect of delivering a sign smaller than usual is to pull the audience closer to the minister—the congregation would be on the edges of their seats, focusing on the minister's hands and body, waiting for the delivery of the next point. This method of signing is similar to that of oral performers who lower their voice to entice the audience to listen more carefully to what comes next. To change the minds and hearts of the deaf students sitting in the chapel, ministers needed their religious rhetoric to reach them through sign language, the deaf students' natural language.

Many ministers and educators argued that sign language was not only a practical means of teaching religion to deaf students but also the only language that would connect to the conscience or soul of the individual. Long claimed that "[s]piritual truths told and explained in the language of signs reach the understanding and conscience of the deaf child to a degree no other means can possibly accomplish."[13] Sign language was capable of expressing the minister's appeals to the deaf students' emotions and conveying the abstract Protestant theology of the sermons. Up until the mid-twentieth century, most ministers in the chapels were following in Thomas Gallaudet's lead and teaching the Gospel to deaf students in residential schools. Protestant ministers wanted the "unsaved" deaf students to become saved and to know God.

With the increase in the separation of religion and education in the early twentieth century partly as a result of nondenominational teaching policies and increasing secularization in society, school publications like the *Silent Worker* indicate that the chapel services at deaf institutions played a significant role in the stabilization of sign language use. In addition, some school brochures and manuals in the first half of the twentieth century suggest the importance of religious training at residential schools for deaf students in the United States.

The *Silent Worker* often included editorials, articles, and stories reprinted from other newspapers on the religious training of deaf students and adults. The *Silent Worker*, like other secular publications for the deaf community, frequently advertised the visits of ministers at state schools and church events. Throughout the early twentieth century, educators and concerned deaf community members wrote about the power of sign language—and only sign language—to reach the conscience of deaf Americans. In 1909 the *Silent Worker* reprinted an editorial by Arthur G. Mashburn, superintendent of the Arkansas Deaf-Mute Institute, in which he stated his belief in the ability of sign language to appeal to the emotions of deaf persons:

> The Sign-language is the natural language of the deaf. It is beautiful, expressive, and graceful. It appeals to the heart of the deaf as no other language can. It is the language of the soul. It stirs the heart to the deepest depths of pathos; it convulses the frame with the merriest peals of laughter. I have seen again and again some mighty Demosthenes of the deaf carry his audience in the sweep of one fleeting moment from the agony of burning tears to the delight of conquered smiles. It appeals to the deaf as nothing else can. It is an easy means of communication.[14]

Mashburn's sentiments, like those of many other educators, were echoed by the president of Gallaudet College, Percival Hall, in 1913. At the School for the Deaf in Jackson, Mississippi, Hall addressed celebrators of "Mississippi Day," referencing the ineffective use of manual spelling:

> Many do not know the difference between signs and manual spelling. They do not realize that the language of signs is a powerful and beautiful language, capable of expressing joy, sadness, despair, hope, love, and a very wide range of ideas. They do not know that for ninety-five years thousands of deaf people in this country have been taught the laws of God and the lesson of Christ by means of the Sign-language so that they have lived clean and honorable lives.[15]

While expressing the cultural values of the deaf community as aligned with Protestant teachings, Hall alluded to the value of sign language to convey the religious teachings of ministers to deaf people. In a simply stated claim that sign language can connect to the deaf people, a 1919 article in the *Silent Worker* states that "there is and always will be more depth and soul and

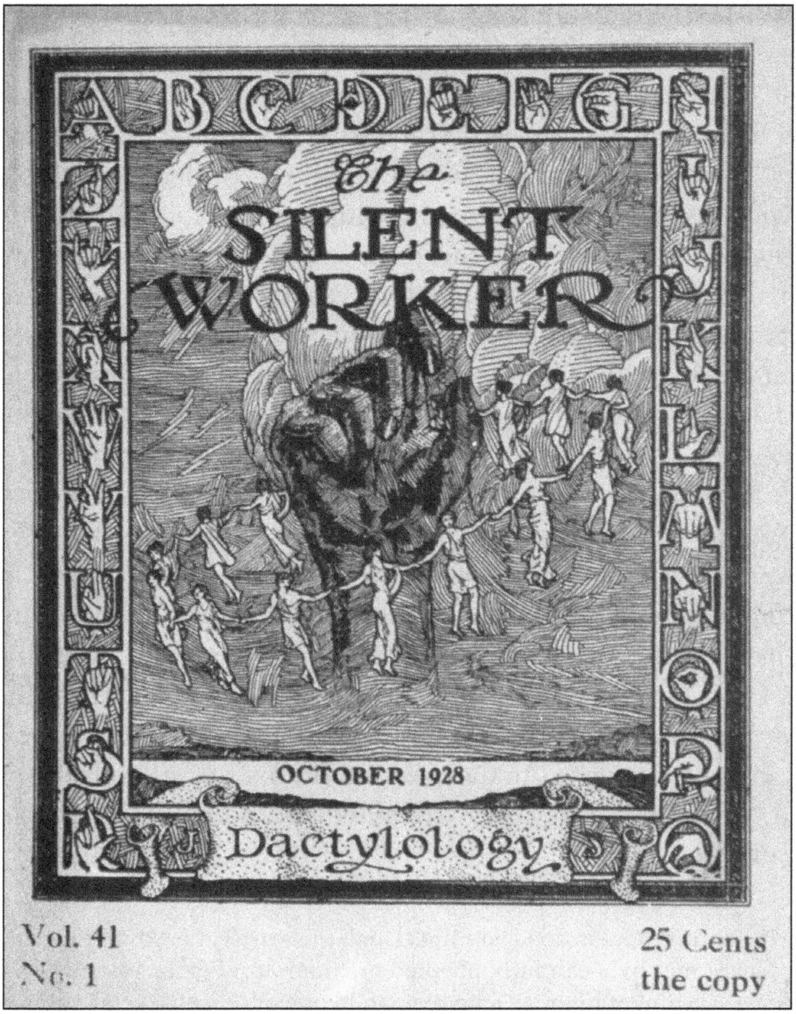

Silent Worker, October 1928 issue. Note the manual alphabet and the print alphabet that surround the page. (Gallaudet University Archives, Washington, DC)

meaning brought [into] their consciousness through the language of signs."[16] Those who supported sign language use in the chapels at residential schools saw not only the practical use of signs but also its effectiveness in fulfilling the ministers' purpose, which was to bring more deaf sinners to God.

While residential schools for deaf children in the early twentieth century promoted religious services by requiring attendance, they were also encouraging the use of sign language and helping to connect deaf students to a growing deaf community. Deaf community leaders ministered to deaf students in chapels using sign language and thus served as role models for many of them. Historian Susan Burch points out that "signed religious instruction created a bridge between students and the outside Deaf community by introducing adult Deaf leaders to Deaf school children."[17] Chapel services introduced deaf students to a deaf community larger than that of their peers at school and suggested a value system for them that was grounded in Protestant theology.

Evidence of this cultural value system in the mid-twentieth century is found in school brochures and manuals. While sifting through materials in the archives at Gallaudet University, I came across a section of school brochures for the New York School for the Deaf. One brochure had a green cover and black-and-white photos inside. It had no date but referenced a 1954 policy allowing girls to attend again. One section of this school brochure, titled "Spiritual Needs Met," explained the school's policy in this regard:

> While the school is nondenominational, the spiritual needs of the pupils are met by a carefully planned program of religious instruction under the direction of a clergyman and lay workers of several faiths. Separate services are conducted one a week for each denomination, and this religious instruction carries over into the religious life of the family, in addition to the religious and social welfare activities of associations and societies for the adult deaf.

The inclusion of this policy is significant. The school clearly states that it is nondenominational but that it will serve the deaf students by offering them religious training. The purpose of the religious instruction is not only to meet the desires of the family of the deaf student but also to prepare students for life after school, in which they will interact with other members of the deaf community. The New York School for the Deaf identifies the place of chapel services and the value of religious training in the lives of older deaf community members, as well as its importance in the lives of its students.

Another publication for the New York School for the Deaf, the 1967 catalog, also suggests the school's role in incorporating religious instruction with deaf education. One black-and-white photograph in particular stands out. Its caption reads, "Lunch-time in the dining area of the building." The subject of the picture is four children and two staff members, all sitting around a table with their heads bowed and hands pressed together in prayer. This picture is interesting for many reasons. While it shows that students and staff members prayed before meals, it also demonstrates that the school values religious practices and encourages them in the deaf students the school serves. This image also suggests that the religious practices are individualized or that the photograph was staged, which is likely. For deaf students to pray together, heads would not be bowed—eyes would be up to see a signer or read the lips of a speaker leading the prayer. In any event, this photo demonstrates a connection between religious values and deaf education well into the twentieth century at state schools for deaf students.

Chapel services at residential schools for deaf students continued to foster a relationship between sign language use and religious instruction. In using sign language in chapel services, schools supported not only the chosen means of communication of many deaf community members but also the community's religious values, which were mainly Protestant ones. Upon graduation, many students found themselves seeking places in ministry or as congregants in Protestant churches, where they could continue to socialize with deaf peers and be ministered to in sign language. The church sanctuary was maintained as a signing place that provided both a social life for adult deaf community members and classes for continued learning after graduation. Because it ministered to the deaf community, the church was a legitimate outgrowth of these schools. The ties between religious teachings and community fellowship were fostered in the school chapels and maintained in sanctuaries beyond the schools.

Safe Signing Places

Because the use of sign language brought many deaf people to church, even Episcopal churches ministered to deaf individuals of different faiths. In 1930, Guilbert Campbell Braddock, minister at St. Ann's Church, stated, "St. Ann's opens its services to all the deaf irrespective of religious affiliations, and it is said the influence of the church thus reaches some 4,000 deaf-mutes in the metropolis."[18] Sign language use and the opportunity to socialize with other sign language users were priorities in selecting a place of worship, not denomination affiliation. As historian Susan Burch notes, "[I]ndependent Deaf churches provided a constant and growing place of sanctuary for religiously minded Deaf people. They helped preserve and transmit sign language as well."[19] Deaf adults found themselves a safe signing place in Protestant churches.

Throughout the deaf community's history, signing churches have played a significant role in providing deaf adults opportunities to socialize. Because of the importance of being around other signers, "deaf people's social life revolves about the church."[20] In 1965, one minister stated that some churches even recruited congregants on this basis: "We recruit our church members from graduates of the state schools for the deaf—those who find themselves unable to go to regular churches for worship, and who fall back upon the sign language for social contacts."[21] The social factor a church plays in the life of a deaf adult cannot be overlooked. In 1961, another writer noted that "[c]hurches for the deaf usually serve as a social center as well as a spiritual center, for deaf persons in widely scattered areas do not often have the chance to get together."[22] While the church provides the deaf congregants and attendees with religious teaching, it is also an important signing place that some writers have compared to recreational activity such as attending movies or signed lectures. In 1919 the *Silent Worker* noted that "[t]he minister in the pulpit who expounds the Gospel in impressive gestures, while his homilies may not be classed as recreation, brings solace and comfort to the deaf wayfarers along the road of life."[23] A preacher may comfort deaf congregants or attendees by what is signed in the sermon, but more than likely the cultural identification a signing preacher presents for a deaf congregant provides far greater comfort, so much so that the commonality of the signed language is of greater importance than the denominational differences that may exist. This characteristic of the deaf community transcends the twentieth century. In 1994 a writer noted that this was evident at one nondenominational church: "At this nondenominational church, the deaf culture ties members together and is stronger than any denominational differences. It's as much a social network for the deaf as it is a place for worship."[24]

The Sanctuary and Sign Language Advocacy

In 1949, the Reverend Arthur G. Leisman, secretary to the Church Workers among the Deaf Conference, wrote the following:

> We encourage Sunday School work in the state schools for the deaf. We endorse the language of signs as the *only* effective means of conveying the Word of God in a church service. We support projects aimed at protecting the rights of the deaf and increasing their sense of security and happiness.[25]

As advocates of sign language use in the church and chapel services in schools for deaf students, these Episcopal ministers helped to not only preserve the language of deaf people but also pave the way to a better life for them after residential school.

Protestant churches helped the deaf community by serving "as centers of welfare and other vital support; Deaf leaders perhaps recognized the need to maintain positive relations with philanthropic organizations that offered such services. . . . Various organizations crossed denominational boundaries, establishing joint effort in Deaf outreach programs and civil rights campaigns."[26]

By the mid-twentieth century, Baptist and Methodist as well as Episcopal churches were the most active in ministering to deaf people.[27] In these sites, meetings were held on subjects relating to the deaf community. For example, in 1974 a meeting to discuss captioned television was held at St. Ann's Church. In addition, an April 1974 bulletin from St. Ann's Church reported that an estimated three hundred people representing the political interests of the deaf community had met with representatives from NBC, CBS, ABC, MetroMedia, PBS, and WNYC. It stated that "[a]ll in all, it appeared to be a very successful beginning" and added that "[w]hat is needed now is for everyone to write to all the various networks supporting the idea of captioning programs, especially news broadcasts." St. Ann's Church advocated the use of captioned television so that deaf individuals could be included in what mainstream America took for granted—access to televised news programs and shows (chapter 4 explores social activism by the deaf community). In sum, the work of the late nineteenth- and twentieth-century churches on behalf of deaf people indicates the deaf community's movement toward political positioning.

The effectiveness of the Protestant church's advocacy for sign language use and for the deaf community in general was due to the leaders who emerged from these ministries:

> Through the Episcopal Church, . . . a succession of men were [*sic*] produced, strong in that they were eminently qualified as leaders among the deaf. These priests and religious workers were notable for the extent to which they participated in the entire social life of the deaf. Not only did they inaugurate the usual social programs in connection with the church (literary societies, men's clubs, guilds) but these clergymen

were called into all the organizations that aimed to promote the welfare of the deaf. They, along with the teachers of the deaf seemed to be the natural leaders—if not the only leaders.[28]

As leaders, these deaf and hearing ministers intertwined their religious callings with the will to serve the deaf community's political interests. The pulpit became a place not only to advocate sign language use through teaching the word of God in the visual language but also to appeal to the interests of the deaf congregants and address the concerns of the deaf community:

> Deaf churches served as bridges between communities and ideas. It is clear from remarks made by both leaders and followers that the spiritual elite used their pulpits to link religious values with Deaf political issues. Often, Deaf ministers and supportive hearing ones took leading roles in major social and political organizations, including the National Fraternal Society of the Deaf.[29]

In the twentieth century, the Protestant churches' efforts to preserve sign language and protect the deaf community's rights had a significant impact. The link of deaf clergy to leadership in secular deaf organizations is also notable. For instance, some ministers assumed leadership roles in the National Association of the Deaf.[30] Whether it was their sense of religious duty or the benevolent roots of the deaf community in the United States, the deaf ministers served the deaf community in more than ministerial capacities.

Conclusion

The work of Protestant chapel and church services not only helped in stabilizing the use of sign language but also provided the deaf community with leaders and advocates that looked after their political interests as well as their spiritual well-being. According to some observers of the role religion played in the deaf community in mid-twentieth-century America, Braddock writes that

> [a] moral and spiritual sense has been developed in them which offsets the lost senses of sight and hearing and which makes a full life and a glorious life possible for these persons. Not only the special schools for the deaf but also the special religious ministrations to the deaf, are responsible for this change in the social status of a once handicapped section of the populace. The deaf have indeed been brought before the Lord.[31]

While the above quote expresses the problematic perspective that the deaf are disabled, the importance of the observation is that church ministries and deaf Americans' participation played a role in changing the social status of the deaf community. Protestant churches for the deaf ushered in leaders of the deaf community who were empowered by their sense of morality and loyalty to their cultural values, particularly the use of sign language. Through the use of sign language, the social functions it played in the lives of deaf adults, the advocacy shown for members of the deaf community, and the emergence of deaf community leaders from it, the Protestant church is a significant component in the history of Deaf culture and the preservation of sign language.

Notes

1. Berg and Buzzard, *Thomas Gallaudet*, 26.
2. Manson, "Work of the Protestant Churches," 394.
3. Ibid., 388.
4. Ibid., 394.
5. Quoted in ibid., 399.
6. "Religion and the Sign Language," 149.
7. Ibid.
8. Sexton, "Religion for the Deaf."
9. Long, *Sign Language*, 20.
10. Ibid.
11. "The Chapel," 136.

12. Mountford, *Gendered Pulpit*, 7.

13. Long, *Sign Language*, 20.

14. Mashburn, "Sign Language," 83.

15. Hall, "Truth about the Deaf, Their Sign Language, and Their Education," 15.

16. "Burden of Deafness," 166.

17. Burch, *Signs of Resistance*, 46.

18. Braddock, quoted in "Gallaudet to Honor Alumnus Who Carries Gospel to Deaf."

19. Burch, *Signs of Resistance*, 46.

20. Knight, "Silent Sermon."

21. Braddock, quoted in ibid.

22. Martin, "Lift Up Your Hands in the Sanctuary and Praise the Lord," 5.

23. "Burden of Deafness," 166.

24. "Deaf Worship."

25. Quoted in Manson, "Work of the Protestant Churches," 398; emphasis added.

26. Burch, *Signs of Resistance*, 48.

27. Sexton, "Religion for the Deaf."

28. Manson, "Work of the Protestant Churches," 388.

29. Burch, *Signs of Resistance*, 49.

30. Manson, "Work of the Protestant Churches," 388.

31. Braddock, "Ye Are Witnesses."

4

Religious Rhetoric in Deaf Community Activism and Advocacy

We'd rather promote the notion of the deaf community as being a language-based culture rather than [a] medically limited community.

—Bill O'Brien, producing director of *Big River: The Adventures of Huckleberry Finn*

AS THE previous chapters explain, residential schools and church sanctuaries provided opportunities for the deaf community to form social groups and to preserve sign language. Emerging from these interactions is a discourse that reflects a pervasive evangelical Protestant influence. The American deaf community has employed religious rhetoric to empower its arguments for the use and advocacy of sign language. Historically, Thomas H. Gallaudet argued that deaf Americans needed sign language in order to know God. Today, deaf activists advocate the use of sign language so that it will become recognized and respected as an identifier of the deaf community. Although not all deaf Americans subscribe to a religion, religious rhetoric is significant in the discourse of deaf community activists.

In this chapter, I argue that the deaf community in the United States employs religious references, themes, and metaphors in sacred and secular contexts to garner support for the deaf community and its use of sign language. I focus on two specific works of social activism that clearly demonstrated to both deaf and hearing audiences the argument for the need to preserve sign language. In the early twentieth and twenty-first centuries, members of the deaf community used mediums that were familiar to both deaf and hearing Americans and demonstrated to the latter that deaf Americans were not unlike them. First, using films, deaf people portrayed themselves as sharing the moral convictions and the (Protestant) religious beliefs of the dominant hearing community in the United States. Then, in the twenty-first-century example I offer, religious rhetoric is used in the content of a larger, secular theater production. In this contemporary context, the deaf community activists use a musical with Protestant themes as a vehicle to persuade hearing audiences to change their ideas about sign language and the deaf community.

Deaf activism, or political activity vigilantly supporting the deaf community by promoting the values of Deaf culture, takes on different forms and uses various media. Barbara Schirmer points out that Deaf culture includes political action.[1] Many facets of the deaf community's activism, often neglected by both rhetoricians and deaf studies scholars, are sites that need to be explored:

> Art forms are also part of the culture. Storytelling has a long tradition in the community. Poetry in the community is performed rather than read. Deaf artists often make their connection with the Deaf community clear in their work, and when they do, it is considered Deaf art.... Deaf theater has a long rich history. . . . Members of the community come together in community social groups, organizations, churches, synagogues, fraternal orders, and sororities.[2]

I contend that the deaf community's historical use of film and its contemporary use of the theater are rich, artful expressions of deaf activism like those that Schirmer lists. Throughout the twentieth century, the deaf community advocated in many instances, politically and socially, for access to American culture, whether it be through captions (first of film and later television), telecommunications (TTY/TDD and video relay) or the Americans with Disabilities Act (ADA). In 1988, the deaf community's activism made national news with the Deaf President Now (DPN) protest at Gallaudet University.

The many examples of the deaf community's social activism are vast. I have selected two examples to highlight because they epitomize a shifting stance in the community's activism—from defensive to offensive—while employing a rhetoric that would move both deaf and hearing audiences. Historically, the films made by the National Association of the Deaf (NAD) to promote and preserve the values of Deaf culture in the United States use religion rhetorically to promote a deaf identity of morally grounded, educated deaf men and women who value sign language. Deaf West Theatre's 2004–2005 national tour of *Big River: The Adventures of Huckleberry Finn* explicitly empowers a deaf identity built on overcoming strife and persuades audience members to change their beliefs and attitudes about the deaf community and its use of sign language. *Big River* is not a representation of the history of the deaf community through its narrative story; however, it is a significant expression of a deaf rhetoric through its production. I contend that both the historical and the contemporary forms of deaf activism are evidence of a link between an oppressed community and its use of religious rhetoric to overcome the stereotypes held by a dominant hearing community while advocating the preservation and use of sign language.

Religious Rhetoric in Deaf Activists' Films

As the number of educated deaf individuals grew, so did support for a national organization to promote the best interests of deaf Americans. In 1880 the National Association of the Deaf was established. The formation of the NAD was the deaf community's response both to the assault on its members by oralists like Alexander Graham Bell and to its belief that deaf people who had been living in different parts of the United States should come together to address their needs. With its long history of such advocacy, the

Clip of George Veditz from the film *The Preservation of the Sign Language.* (Gallaudet University Archives, Washington, DC)

NAD has effectively sought to preserve and promote the values of Deaf culture. In the late nineteenth and early twentieth centuries, the NAD fought for the right of deaf people to drive, investigated and battled discriminatory hiring practices, condemned deaf beggars for giving the deaf community a bad reputation, and resisted the banishment of sign language.[3] In response to the oralists' attempts to eliminate sign language, the NAD began its moving picture campaign in 1910.[4] George W. Veditz was mainly responsible for the NAD's filming of master signers.[5] Veditz, highly respected in the deaf community, was a Deaf rights activist: "After graduating from Gallaudet in 1884 with record-setting high grades, [Veditz] became an outspoken advocate for the rights of Deaf people."[6] As president of the NAD from 1904 to 1910, Veditz campaigned for the NAD's moving picture fund to "record, preserve, and promote the use of Sign Language during a period when the domination of a strictly oralist approach to instruction threatened the use of sign language in schools for Deaf students."[7] To protect the deaf community from the oralists' threats, both hearing and deaf leaders turned to film.

Popular moving pictures reached both hearing and deaf audiences because the films were silent and produced with captions and simple plots. In addition, deaf performers sometimes had roles in the earliest recorded films: "One of the first moving pictures, produced in 1902 by American Mutoscope and Biograph Company, showed a deaf woman signing the 'Star-Spangled Banner.'"[8] And Deaf actor Granville Redmond had a role in several of Charlie Chaplin's silent films.[9] To preserve sign language, the deaf community also filmed poems, lectures, and stories delivered by master signers.[10] One such film is "Memories of Old Hartford," by John Burton Hotchkiss, a graduate of both the American School for the Deaf and Gallaudet College. Hotchkiss went on to become the first deaf teacher at Gallaudet College.[11] In his signed history of the founding of the first permanent school for the deaf in the United States, Hotchkiss describes in great detail his mentor, Laurent Clerc.[12] Hotchkiss shares his memory of Clerc by recollecting his physical characteristics as well as his devotion to educating deaf people.[13] Films became a vehicle to capture and distribute the history, folklore, and discourse of the deaf community in the United States to both hearing and deaf audiences. The NAD's films were circulated throughout the deaf community through residential schools, social clubs, and churches, ensuring that future generations would know deaf history.[14] Recognizing the value in reaching both hearing and deaf audiences, the NAD raised funds from 1910 to 1920 to create films that captured their language, persuaded audiences to back their community, and garnered support for the use of sign language.

One of the first master signers to be filmed was Edward Miner Gallaudet, who "enjoyed national recognition as the most recognized advocate for Deaf rights."[15] As a hearing child of a deaf mother and the son of Thomas H. Gallaudet, Edward M. Gallaudet learned sign language early in life and used it throughout his career as the superintendent of the elite Gallaudet College. He was greatly influenced by the benevolence of his Protestant father, and, like him, he served the deaf community through his leadership. As mentioned in chapter 2, Edward M. Gallaudet spearheaded the drive to establish a college solely for deaf Americans, where they could achieve certificates and degrees in higher learning. He also argued on an international level for the preservation of sign language and signed stories and speeches for the NAD's film project.

Like E. M. Gallaudet, other hearing deaf community leaders joined deaf role models, including "Gallaudet professors John B. Hotchkiss and Amos G. Draper; . . . the deaf principal of the New York School for the Deaf at Fanwood, Thomas F. Fox; Robert P. McGregor, first president of the NAD; George T. Dougherty, a deaf chemist; and a deaf Episcopal priest, James H. Cloud,"[16] as filmed signers of speeches, stories, or histories. Among both hearing and deaf signers, the themes for these presentations were often nationalism, religion, or stories ("oral" histories).[17] In the United States, the rhetorical use of religion, such as the filming of master signers signing "The Lord's Prayer," was a convention in deaf community discourse to persuade audiences that the deaf community could be identified by its religious practices. Religious rhetoric also reinforced the similarities between the deaf community and the dominant Protestant society of the early twentieth century. Historian Susan Burch points out that "The Lord's Prayer" was frequently signed on film by master signers.[18]

One reason for this selection was the prayer's familiarity to both hearing and deaf audiences. The master signers could thus assume their audiences would know it by heart, so attaching the words they knew to the signs they saw in the film would help them understand how signs convey meaning and are used to construct a language.

These religious themes also presented morality as a value of the emerging Deaf culture. Sermons filmed in sign language and shown to a broad audience of both deaf and hearing people demonstrated that the deaf community lacked neither God nor morals; its members were civilized men and women, often of elite standing, and highly educated (usually at Gallaudet College). Appealing to audiences that shared its religious ideology, the discourse of the deaf community included evangelical Protestant rhetoric to convince audiences to support the deaf community's values, primarily the place of sign language in the education and lives of deaf Americans.

The use of religious topics, as captured on the NAD films that were publicized by Veditz, served to promote an American deaf identity that was educated, moral, and willing to serve the community by educating others about its values. The emerging deaf identity presented in the NAD's films was in contrast to that assigned by opponents of sign language, who argued that all deaf students should be educated using oralist methods.[19] These films of master signers served the deaf community by advancing the value of sign language through the use of religious themes and metaphors in their lectures and stories.

Veditz rhetorically employed religion especially to advocate the preservation of sign language. His famous filmed speech, *Preservation of the Sign Language*,[20] was made in 1913, when oralists were gaining ground. The film was viewed at churches and social halls by both deaf and hearing audiences.[21] As a powerful signer and rhetor, Veditz carefully analyzed his audience, who also val-

Granville Redmond with Charlie Chaplin in 1917. (Courtesy of The Irvine Museum, in Memory of Mildred Albronda)

ued religion, before he selected the signs that would convey his passionate message. In front of a curtained background, Veditz evokes biblical rhetoric to condemn the oralists. He cites the oralists' drive to ban sign language from every facet of the deaf community: "They have tried to banish signs from the schoolroom, from the churches, and from the earth."[22] By calling the oralists " 'false prophets' who proclaim 'that the American way of teaching the deaf is a mistake,' "[23] Veditz depicts them as heartless and truly uninformed about sign language and deaf people. He claims that the oralists, who are " 'A new race of pharaohs that knew not Joseph' are now taking over the land and many of our American schools."[24] By referring to the oralists as "pharaohs that knew not Joseph," Veditz emphasizes their lack of benevolence, a striking contrast to the Gallaudets, who served the deaf community through their Protestant kindness and advocated the use and recognition of sign language in the school, the sanctuary, and the social lives of the deaf community. He evokes the struggles of the Israelites, who lost the protection of their more compassionate ruler after Joseph died. The Israelites went on to face slavery under the new rulers or pharaohs. According to Veditz, the oralists would enslave deaf students by forcing them to learn speech and forbidding them to sign.

Just as Veditz's fiery biblical rhetoric separates the oralists from the manualists, he incites the deaf community through religious rhetoric. He concludes his passionate presentation by signing, "It is my hope that we all will love and guard our beautiful sign language as the noblest gift God has given to deaf people."[25] Veditz's reference to sign language as "a gift from God" invokes a responsibility on the part of deaf Americans to preserve and promote sign language and to even maintain its beauty through proper use. He argued that the graciousness of deaf Americans should be visible in their signs. The implication is that God created sign language; therefore, continuing to sign would be putting God's creation to good use. If God created sign language, it would also mean that those who opposed it would be enemies or even doing the devil's work. Veditz's filmed presentation is an example of graceful signing and a vigorous defense of the deaf community's values, which included the belief that the use of sign language demonstrated their moral identity: They would use God's creation of sign language to gain salvation, thus sharing a Protestant ideology with the dominant hearing society.

The NAD films underscore the American deaf community's use of religious rhetoric to promote the preservation of sign language. For the early twentieth-century deaf community leaders, religious rhetoric was deaf activists' rhetoric. The master signers' biblical references and metaphors captured in NAD's moving pictures tied sign language use and thus a deaf identity to Protestantism.

Amplifying the Gap: Twentieth-Century Deaf Activism

In addition to the NAD's advocacy, the deaf community garnered attention through other moments of activism in the twentieth century, some of which were overtly tied to religion and religious rhetoric. However, in many cases, we see a community responding to an apparent gap in media access—telecommunication, film, television—or in consideration of its members' ability to be intelligent and capable leaders—the Deaf President Now protest, for instance. These moments of activism amplify the separation that occurred and still occurs between the deaf and the hearing communities.

Some of this activism continued to occur in the sanctuary as more and more churches began recognizing the deaf congregant. Throughout the early twentieth century, church organizations of different denominations developed ministries to deaf Americans. Although the Episcopal Church took the lead in deaf ministers and deaf congregations, others soon followed. Lutheran, Methodist, Baptist, Latter Day Saints, Jewish, and Catholic ministries began serving deaf people throughout the United States. As more and more clergy desired to work with the deaf community, "an increasing number of seminaries began adding sign language to their curricula."[26] Interpreters played a key role in providing deaf congregants access to churches. Because of them, deaf congregants were and still are able to worship alongside hearing congregants. Many religious interpreters have been children of deaf adults and are quite skilled.[27] To this day, church interpreters are often volunteers who are visible reminders to hearing congregations of the language gap that exists for the deaf worshippers at a hearing church. Also, it is often churches that offer free sign language classes to their community members. The Southern Baptist Convention devotes a segment of its work to serving deaf people nationally and internationally through the Southern Baptist Conference. The work of the church in preserving sign language is still evident in the twenty-first century.[28]

As interpreters and ministers helped deaf community members worship in their own language, the deaf community has battled a greater gap in access to film, television, and telecommunications. The early films of the 1900s offered deaf and hearing audiences alike a common entertainment experience. Because the films were silent and captions interspersed throughout, they were accessible to both deaf and hearing audiences. With the arrival of "talkies" in 1927, deaf audiences were excluded. Not until twenty years later did a not-so-successful attempt at captioning occur.[29] A more successful venture occurred from 1949 to 1958 using a technique by a Belgian company to etch captions right on the film's finished print.[30] "Captioned Films for the Deaf" was a not-for-profit initiative that captioned and distributed Hollywood films to schools for deaf children but eventually ran out of money and encountered challenges by the industry related to film piracy. As a result, legislation was passed to assign the Office of Education, Bureau of Education for the Handicapped of the U.S. Department of Health, Education, and Welfare, to caption and distribute films for deaf Americans. The late 1950s were thus a time of growth for captioned films, which eventually influenced the movement for captions for television broadcasts.

In 1964 deaf electronic scientist Robert Weitbrecht developed an acoustic coupler that made the telephone accessible to deaf people. Weitbrecht made it possible to use teletypewriters with telephones to send and receive text messages. Logistical, financial, and technical challenges were confronted and dealt with before the widespread use of the TTY in the mid-1980s.[31] Advancements in technology and telecommunications enabled deaf people to stay in touch in easier, quicker, and more convenient ways. By using TTYs or a telecommunications device for deaf people (TDD), the deaf community could more easily organize, thereby positively affecting their political activities.

Debates regarding "open" (i.e., cannot be turned on or off by viewers) and "closed" captioning (i.e., newer technology that allows individuals to elect captioning to be on) occupied the 1970s. In 1979, three major television networks agreed to offer several hours a week of closed-captioning broadcasts: "five hours each for ABC and NBC, and twelve and a half hours for PBS."[32] In the 1980s, deaf people had more access to television through captioning, but many hours of broadcasting were still not captioned. In 1989 the "decoder chip bill" was introduced into the Senate with explanations of its value to the deaf community and as a literacy tool. People were using closed captioning to improve their vocabulary and reading skills.[33] Celebrities advocated for closed captioning in House of Representatives hearings by the Energy and Commerce Committee's Telecommunications and Finance Subcommittee to garner support for the decoder chip bill. More celebrities came out for the Senate hearings. These famous persons were members of the deaf community, many of whom were culturally Deaf. Their personal experiences and anecdotes pointed out the advantages of closed captioning and the need for its wide accessibility, which could be achieved by requiring the decoder chip to automatically be installed in televisions rather than requiring a separate decoder box to be purchased. Not until the 1990s were captioning mandates in place. The Decoder Circuitry Act unanimously passed the Senate on August 2, 1990, and was signed into law on October 15, 1990, "requiring all televisions manufactured or imported into America with screens thirteen inches or larger to be capable of displaying closed captions as of July 1, 1993."[34]

Part of the success of the debates surrounding closed captioning and the decoder chip bill can be attributed specifically to the general awareness of the deaf community, which was one result of the 1988 Deaf President Now (DPN) protest.[35] The week of March 6–13, 1988, was one of protest and momentous events that became known as "the civil rights movement of deaf people."[36] A long history of being ignored or considered inferior was amplified on March 6, 1988, when Gallaudet University's board of trustees appointed another hearing president when viable deaf candidates were in their hiring pool. Students, alumni, and faculty marched through the streets of Washington, DC, to the Mayflower Hotel, where the board had convened, to express their outrage at the decision. This action kicked off a week of deaf revolution. Students and supporters closed down the campus for seven days, thereby educating the world about their fortitude and willingness to fight to be recognized as a minority that deserved to be led by one of its own.

Building on the civil rights rhetoric that preceded it, the DPN protest positioned the deaf community as worthy of receiving recognition and fair treatment. As the national and international news began to cover the events unfolding at Gallaudet University, supporters from all areas of life came forward. Organizations pledged their support to the students, politicians commented on the powerful message the students' protest conveyed, and civil rights leaders favored a deaf president. The Reverend Jesse L. Jackson declared that "[t]he problem is not that the students do not hear. The problem is that the hearing world does not listen."[37] The deaf community, through DPN, educated a nation in a very short time about all that deaf people are capable of, especially the fact that they can decide for themselves what is best.

On March 11, 1988, six days into the protest, the newly appointed president, Dr. Elisabeth Zinser, resigned, fulfilling one of the protesters' demands. On Sunday, March 13, 1988, I. King Jordan was announced as the first deaf president of Gallaudet University. The American deaf community clearly demonstrated that, after years of hearing people making decisions for them, they were quite capable of deciding for themselves. Even though the DPN protest was located in an educational environment, it articulated much more than issues related to deaf education. It also empowered community members to make changes in their own actions and advocacy and altered the hearing world's ignorant perceptions of deaf people's capabilities and language. Deaf

At the U.S. Capitol, Gallaudet students wave a Deaf President Now banner. (Gallaudet University Archives, Washington, DC)

rhetoric emerged in this revolution, aligning it with civil rights rhetoric and the Protestant theology of overcoming. Poignantly, it was a faculty member who succinctly summed up the protest: "God made the world in seven days, and we changed it in seven days."[38]

The battles the deaf community engaged in to gain access to film, telecommunications, and television were fought defensively. In contrast, the DPN protest is a very clear moment of deaf activism when deaf people reacted en masse to a patronizing decision made for them by hearing people and worked together to change it.

With the empowerment of the deaf community through their successes in the DPN protest, we see them emerge offensively. Rather than being positioned to react to something done to them, the deaf community moves to a stance that educates others in order to make a case for their language and culture.

The Empowerment of the Deaf Community through Theater

The DPN protest clearly demonstrates values of the deaf community. Other public events and forms of expression also serve to promote its values. One example is the Deaf West Theatre production of *Big River: The Adventures of Huckleberry Finn,* which is a musical based on Mark Twain's *Adventures of Huckleberry Finn* and contains religious themes and references. With *Big River,* Deaf West has educated audiences about the struggles that the American deaf community faces while promoting a deaf identity that valorizes sign language. Along with many of the performances on its national tour, Deaf West held information sessions and lectures on the making of *Big River.* For teachers it also provided online materials about *Big River* and the deaf community to encourage classroom discussions about sign language and deaf people. Like the early deaf community leaders who preserved and promoted community values such as sign language use, on film, Deaf West Theatre's production of *Big River* uses a familiar American story with Protestant themes to highlight the plight and transformation of deaf Americans. Before examining the Protestant themes of the production, I offer some background on Deaf West and the making of *Big River.*

It is important to remember that the deaf community of the late nineteenth and early twentieth centuries faced the oralists' attempts to banish sign language and defended their right to use sign language. I argue that since that time the American deaf community has shifted from a defensive stance to an offensive one in which sign language functions as artful expression that appeals to both deaf and hearing audiences. Using both deaf and hearing actors simultaneously, Deaf West Theatre's *Big River* is an example of new activism within the deaf community and an effective means of conveying its empowerment in a secular context.

Deaf community leaders use different forms of expression to promote the values of the deaf community. Ed Waterstreet and his wife, Linda Bove,[39] both Deaf,[40] established Deaf West Theatre in California in 1991. Waterstreet and Bove understand Deaf West Theatre as having a mission to spread the message that Deaf culture has overcome threats to its very existence and become a thriving community that includes culturally enriching theater experiences:

> The mission of Deaf West Theatre is to improve and enrich the cultural lives of Los Angeles' two million deaf and hard of hearing citizens, and to produce quality theatre for hearing and deaf audiences. . . . Deaf West seeks to create, share, and preserve a "legacy of deaf culture" through its Sign Language theatre programs.[41]

With *Big River*, Deaf West has created a bicultural (hearing and deaf) theater experience that serves to educate audiences who may have been unfamiliar with Deaf culture (primarily hearing audiences) or with musical theater (primarily deaf audiences). Both deaf and hearing audiences are provided access to this theatrical experience. Waterstreet claims that "[n]ow, deaf and hard of hearing audiences can fully identify with characters who break into song or, in our case, sign, where normal dialogue cannot contain emotions, and the language becomes more heightened and poetic. This is the kind of access that we have been heretofore denied."[42]

Deaf West advocates for full inclusion by offering entertainment to both hearing and deaf audiences simultaneously.

Inclusive Theater Experience: Simultaneous Communication

Deaf West Theatre's production of *Big River* is an adaptation of an adaptation. Based on Mark Twain's *Adventures of Huckleberry Finn*, the musical was first presented in 1984 at the American Repertory Theater in Cambridge, Massachusetts. On April 25, 1985, it opened on Broadway and won that year's Tony award for best musical. Los Angeles's Deaf West Theatre reinvented *Big River* in fall 2001, using American Sign Language (ASL) and deaf and hearing actors. A year later, it was presented again as a coproduction between Deaf West Theatre and the Mark Taper Forum before opening on Broadway in summer 2003. The last show on Broadway to include hearing and deaf actors was the play *Children of a Lesser God*, which ran from 1980 to 1982.[43] In summer 2004, Deaf West Theatre launched their national tour of *Big River*.

Deaf West Theatre's production of *Big River* is unique because it combines deaf and hearing actors to tell a story with many levels of significance. Hearing actors speak and sing while signing. Deaf actors sign their dialogue and songs while hearing actors are used to speak and sing the signed parts of deaf actors. For example, the character Huck Finn is played by a deaf actor who uses sign language. His dialogue and songs are narrated and sung by the character Mark Twain, played by a hearing actor. The hearing actor who is speaking and singing the signed part of a deaf actor is always on stage, in full costume, and is visible but does not distract from the performance of the deaf actor. When referring to directing a cast of hearing and deaf actors signing and singing, director and choreographer Jeff Calhoun claims that "[i]f a Broadway show is a jigsaw puzzle with 20 pieces, this is a jigsaw puzzle with 350 pieces."[44] As a hearing director, Calhoun had to adapt staging, direction, and costuming to work with the actors signing. To see visual cues, deaf actors needed to be spaced on the stage unobstructed by staging or other actors, props and costuming needed to allow actors to sign uninhibitedly, and all signing needed to be readable by deaf audiences. *Big River* is a work that advances Deaf culture and, like Veditz's activism with the NAD, promotes the use of sign language through biblical references and themes.

Deaf West's *Big River* is an example of how deaf community activists employ rhetorical strategies to convey the value of sign language with the purpose of changing the thoughts and behaviors of audience members who are unfamiliar with or think little of the deaf community. Deaf West offers a theater experience that is an art form capable of reaching an audience that may be unfamiliar with the values (specifically the recognition and use of sign language) of the American deaf community. Sign language is used in a theatrical way in *Big River* to achieve a translation that conveys Twain's humor to a deaf audience. Bill O'Brien, who is the producing director for *Big River*, actively participated in the sign language translation of the production. The hearing actors cast in *Big River* studied with master signers to train in ASL. O'Brien claims that all of the sign language translations are

> very meticulously done. . . . It isn't just signed English. We try to exploit sign language to its fullest. . . . That means the humor of Twain is going to be communicated and understood by the deaf actor and by the deaf audience and by the hearing audience and the hearing actors. We're all laughing at the same joke, we're all understanding and learning the same thing about the characters and the relationships. It's a very involved process.[45]

Some audience members may be skeptical about the ability of ASL to function as a language and convey the same messages as spoken language. O'Brien articulates the effort that went into creating a performance that would simultaneously convey equivalent messages to deaf and hearing audiences in two different languages, providing full inclusion. This method of performance makes Deaf West's production different from typical theater performances.

The theater experience that Deaf West provides is different from that of most hearing theaters, which offer a set number of performances that are interpreted for deaf individuals in the audience. At such performances, the interpreters are often standing off to one side of the stage. The deaf members of the audience then must look back and forth between the interpreter and the performance. Moreover, the interpreters necessarily lag slightly behind the performance. First the interpreter listens to what is being voiced and then translates the information into sign language. Often the deaf audience receives the information a few seconds or more after the hearing members of the audience.

Deaf West provides a theater experience that allows both deaf and hearing audiences to enjoy the same performance without interpreters. The deaf and hearing actors of Deaf West collaborate to communicate the story and effectively convey a deeper message about bicultural understanding—not just between the black slaves and the white characters but also between the deaf and the hearing characters. One critic states that "Mark Twain's *Huckleberry Finn* is elevated in this stunning revival to an almost holy plane. Blending hearing and deaf actors into the most responsive ensemble you can imagine, the show becomes a celebration of human communication and the striving together to achieve it."[46] Deaf West's rhetorical strategy demonstrates the complementary way in which deaf and hearing people can work together to achieve a specific purpose or, in the case of *Big River*, multiple purposes. Deaf West entertains an audience, certainly, but it also appeals to a broader audience because of its combination of language use.

Through the performance of *Big River*, Deaf West serves the deaf community by educating others about its battle to preserve sign language. Waterstreet and Bove take their mission seriously. As mentioned earlier, Deaf West's website provided teaching materials on the themes in *Big River* as well as the history of deaf Americans. Also, included with some of the dates of the national tour were opportunities for audiences to learn about Deaf West Theatre's history and the making of *Big River*. Waterstreet and Bove offered presentations and question-and-answer sessions for audiences. In doing so, they demonstrated the continuing need to educate others about the deaf community, specifically about its historic experiences as outcasts oppressed by oralists and more recent experiences as professionals offering entertainment to both the deaf and the hearing communities through sign language. The production of *Big River*, the outreach of Waterstreet and Bove, and the supplemental teaching materials suggest that Deaf West recognizes that the dominant hearing society may still view the deaf community as outsiders who are not complete people because they cannot hear.

Deaf West Theatre is also educating audience members about the value of sign language to the deaf community by offering entire productions in sign language combined with voicing. For many hearing audience members, this may be their first exposure to seeing sign language performed by deaf people. As discussed in previous chapters, the American deaf community has struggled to have sign language recognized and accepted as its common language. Deaf Americans share a history of often being viewed and treated as outcasts. In contrast, Deaf West's *Big River* successfully blends Twain's theme of outsiders with the historic struggles of the deaf community to advocate for full inclusion, echoing the current arguments in deaf education, such as those that promote the bilingual-bicultural approach rather than mainstreaming (see the introduction). The theme of outsider is significant because, in Deaf West's production, Huck Finn is an outsider not only because his way of thinking does not always align with that of the Protestant society surrounding him but also because he is deaf.

Protestant Themes in Twain's *Adventures of Huckleberry Finn*

Because *Big River* is an adaptation of *Adventures of Huckleberry Finn*, it is important to briefly look at Twain's original work, which reveals Protestant influences. Many Twain scholars have written about the role religion played in Twain's life—from his attendance at Sunday school as a child to his long friendship with Congregational minister Joe Twichell.[47] Most of these scholars note that throughout Twain's life he battled with his own theology, and these struggles were often played out in his writing.[48] For Twain, his writings were sermons working through his own beliefs and observations. Twain scholar Stanley Brodwin writes, "[A]t the heart of his comic imagination there dwelt the impulses of a preacher, a 'preacher-manqué,' to be sure, because or in spite of a radical predilection to test his own theological and cultural values against the entrenched contradictions he encountered in everyday experience."[49] Though a "frustrated preacher," Twain intertwined his Christian "*counter*theology"[50] with his comic stories quite effectively. Twain maintained that a balance of teaching and preaching would sustain his success as a writer:

> Humor must not professedly teach, and it must not professedly preach, but it must do both if it would live forever. By forever, I mean thirty years. . . . I have always preached. That is the reason I have lasted thirty years. If the humor came of its own accord and uninvited, I have allowed it a place in my sermon, but I was not writing the sermon for the sake of the humor. I would have written the sermon just the same, whether any humor applied for admission or not.[51]

Although his sermon is not typical for a Protestant minister, Twain's conflict with his conscience and the Protestant teachings surrounding him are demonstrated in *Huckleberry Finn*, where Twain challenges Protestant beliefs rather than trying to convert audiences to them.

As a self-described preacher, Twain wrote the story of Huck Finn, an orphaned boy who struggles with the conflict posed by his own conscience and that of the society that has taken him in. Huck learns from his guardians, Widow Douglas and Miss Watson, about the Protestant faith. The widow shows Huck Christian benevolence by taking care of him, and Miss Watson ministers to Huck by encouraging him to choose the path of salvation and stop swearing and smoking. Pap Finn abandons Huck, only to come back to him when he hears that Huck has found a substantial sum of money. While in drunken stupors, Pap abuses Huck to the point that Huck fakes his own death and runs away. Pap is the antithesis of Huck's innocence. He symbolizes the darkness in the society surrounding Huck. Huck sees his path with Miss Watson as restricted and his path with Pap as controlling. He is most free when he runs away and is on the river with Jim, Miss Watson's slave. As Huck travels down the Mississippi River with Jim, their adventures test Huck's beliefs and their friendship. Jim's superstitious readings offer Huck another way of viewing the world—one that contradicts Miss Watson's Protestant beliefs and even those of his abusive father. As Huck is challenged to make decisions based on what is right and wrong, he considers the teachings of the society that has taken him in and struggles with an inner conflict. In the end Huck is transformed only in the sense that he is redeemed by his own true beliefs that counter those of Protestant America, in which he lives: He resists the sins of society and listens to his conscience, which tells him to help free Jim, Miss Watson's "property." Huck makes a decision for himself.

Through Huck Finn, Twain offers readers a character who questions deep-rooted assumptions about "America's providential mission"—freedom through choosing the path of salvation—and offers in their place "a dynamically subversive comic 'theology.'"[52] This theology asks readers to ponder what it means to be free by examining their own conscience when it comes to ingrained assumptions about our culture and society. Huck's dilemma is found in his battle to reconcile Jim's status as "property" belonging to Miss Watson with his view of Jim as a friend and protector. Huck is taught a theology based on the Protestant conviction that sinning is wrong. In this society Huck would be sinning if he did not turn Jim in as a runaway slave. However, Huck recognizes the duplicity of Jim as an outsider of society and as a man, a human being with thoughts, feelings, and goals the same as Huck. For Huck to make the right choice and do the right thing means he must do what society considers wrong—he will try to protect Jim. Huck finds his personal freedom in his choice to follow his conscience, which is in opposition to the Protestant society that has raised him but, because of his orphaned status, views him as an outsider.

Educating Others about the Deaf Community

In Deaf West Theatre's *Big River* Huck's outsider status is heightened by the explicit significance of his deafness, not just his status as an orphan. While the musical maintains Twain's challenge to Protestantism, Huck's deafness introduces another aspect of what it means to be free. Historically, deaf Americans have faced a hearing community that has often made decisions affecting them. Just as there are examples of benevolent hearing people making decisions based on the best interests of the deaf community, there have also been many hearing individuals who have hurt the deaf community. One example, of course, is the oralists, such as Alexander Graham Bell, who sought to banish sign language. This historical oppression of the American deaf community is a lens through which audiences can view *Big River* and understand the significance of Huck's action to make his own decision—an expression of his freedom.

Deaf West's *Big River* is an example of a secular art form containing religious themes and references that serve as tools of deaf activism by supporting and projecting a successful deaf community. The ingrained Protestant influence on Twain, as evident in *Adventures of Huckleberry Finn*, is also present in Deaf West's *Big River*. Deaf West employs a theatrical approach as a rhetorical strategy to reach many audiences with its advocacy of the recognition and use of sign language. Intertwining with Twain's Protestant themes, Deaf West tells the story of not only Huck, who is on a spiritual journey, but also of the deaf community, which was once placed in a defensive position and is now educating others about its members' skills and values in an offensive position.

Deaf West's production of *Big River* is not intended to be a religious exploration of the Protestant influence on the deaf community. However, in the foreground of the musical is the text, which is heavily influenced by Twain's "*counter*theology," so religious themes are evident. Through lyrics and dialogue that reflect religious references to benevolence, redemption, and freedom, Deaf West's *Big River* appeals to the audience's knowledge of early America and the struggles for equality. *Big River*'s content appeals to the audience's emotions and moves the members of the audience to not only identify with the conflict in Huck but to also recognize the struggles the deaf community has endured as outsiders. Deaf West's *Big River* can be interpreted in the context not only of early American struggles with slavery but also of an American deaf community that employs religious rhetoric in its discourse, as evident in the deaf characters.

When Deaf West Theatre decided to create a production of *Big River*, it was given an opportunity to examine the story's themes in the context of the American deaf community. Twain sets up a story that looks at the personal, physical, and political struggles of two different individuals, both outsiders, as told from Huck's perspective. Twain uses the everyday speech of Southern rural whites and blacks to tell Huck's story. Deaf West's production of *Big River* uses the sign language of the American deaf community to convey the important themes in Twain's original work. Linguist Carol A. Padden, a Deaf ASL signer and professor of communications at the University of California at San Diego claims that

> *Big River* teaches us about the struggle for equality in the U.S. Likewise ASL on the stage reminds deaf people of their long struggle for acceptance of their language. . . . For years until the middle of the [twentieth] century, many educators believed that sign languages were "primitive" and "backwards," and that deaf children should learn only through the "oral method," or through speech alone. Many deaf adults today tell stories about being punished for signing secretly with their friends, or being put in classes for the less gifted because they struggled to learn to speak.[53]

Padden's words were included in the playbill for the 2002 Los Angeles performances of *Big River*, allowing the audience a perspective from the deaf community from which to view the production. This information, combined with the deaf-hearing theater experience, allows audiences to gain a better understanding of the deaf community's struggles to preserve sign language. The question-and-answer sessions also demonstrated that *Big River* was educating audiences about the importance of sign language. At one such session I attended in New York, a hearing member of the audience stood up and asked the deaf actors, "Do you really understand everything done on the hands like that? It is incredible." Unfamiliar with sign language and the deaf community, this audience member began to understand the fact that ASL is a complete language. Deaf West Theatre serves the deaf community by educating others about the trials and tribulations the deaf community has endured to retain its language and identity. Because of the early deaf community leaders' activism, sign language has survived, and in works like Deaf West's *Big River* we see it flourishing.

Underlying Protestant Themes in *Big River:* The History of the American Deaf Culture

For audiences, Deaf West's *Big River* serves as a testimony to the successes in the American deaf community. To look back and see what the deaf community has come through is for us to acknowledge and appreciate where it is now. We must also acknowledge the means that Deaf West has chosen to convey its message. As a whole, the production demonstrates that the use of sign language does not impede social development and that it does not prevent people from being "normal," as many oralists argued (and probably many audience members believe). Deafness is still often viewed as a deficit—the lack of hearing. However, the use of sign language in *Big River* symbolizes the positive view of deafness as an equal counterpart to hearing.

The use of sign language by Deaf West, combined with Twain's reference to deafness in his original work,[54] opens up possible analyses from a Deaf perspective. By analyzing Deaf West's *Big River* using a Deaf lens, significant layers of meaning are added to the overall themes of benevolence, redemption, and freedom found in the musical. References to the intertwining of deaf education and the spiritual status of deaf students, the oralists' hold over sign language and the deaf community, and the empowerment the deaf community found in its own experiences all surface when one examines Deaf West's *Big River* in this way. The Protestant themes and references that emerge in *Big River* then present a Deaf activist's rhetoric, one that is clearly religious.

Benevolence: Salvation through Literacy

As outsiders, Huck and Jim experience adventures that highlight the original Christian themes of benevolence, redemption, and freedom, which Twain wrote about in *Adventures of Huckleberry*

Finn. Big River opens with Huck, an uneducated orphan without a home, encountering the benevolence of Protestant society when he is welcomed into the home of the Widow Douglas and her sister, Miss Watson, both of whom represent civilized society. They encourage Huck to go to school and to read his Bible, but Huck would rather go on adventures and seek freedom away from the structure of society, not within the surrounding Protestant belief system. *Big River* opens with the cast signing and singing to Huck the song "Do Ya Wanna Go to Heaven?" Miss Watson and Judge Thatcher scold Huck with signs pointing toward him: "You better learn to read and you better learn your writin' / Or you'll never get to heaven 'cause you won't know how."[55] In *Big River* Huck is admonished by the society that has adopted him and shown him kindness by offering what it perceives is a better life. Huck had better change and learn to read and write, or he will go down the path of damnation, according to his Protestant caregivers.

In *Big River* Huck struggles to believe in something and is surrounded by Widow Douglas and Miss Watson, signing and singing: "You may think that the whole thing is silly / But it ain't silly really and I'll tell you right now / If you don't learn to read, then you can't read your Bible / And you'll never get to heaven 'cause you won't know how."[56] The structured society represented in these lyrics and firm signs teaches Huck he has two choices in life: to follow the path of damnation or the path of salvation. He struggles with which path to take, acting ambivalent yet conflicted. Although the actions of Miss Watson and Widow Douglas may be interpreted as benevolent—trying to help an orphan boy who is less fortunate than they—Huck does not make any definitive decision in their presence.

Huck, portrayed as a deaf boy, battles the conflicts he has with the Protestant faith. Miss Watson and Judge Thatcher's concern for Huck's eternal well-being echoes the work of T. H. Gallaudet among deaf Americans. As mentioned in chapter 1, one reason the first American school for deaf children opened in 1817 was that Hartford community leaders believed that they needed to be educated and learn a language so they could become Christians. These leaders, including T. H. Gallaudet, saw their actions as a ministry to deaf individuals in the United States. Gallaudet believed his actions were benevolent; as part of his Protestant beliefs, he was commissioned to help those less fortunate than he. Like Miss Watson's and Judge Thatcher's encouragement of Huck to learn to read and write, Gallaudet felt compelled to teach deaf students a language so they, too, could know God and not suffer eternal damnation. In *Big River* the theme of benevolence echoes the work of early deaf community leaders. The activism of the Gallaudets and Veditz to secure schools and preserve a language for deaf people came from the Protestant practice of protecting deaf individuals and the emerging deaf community. These deaf activists used a distinct method of discourse that employed religious motives, metaphors, and biblical references to advocate the use of sign language.

Despite the efforts of deaf community leaders like the Gallaudets and Veditz, the deaf community fell under the oppression of oralists. Educators, parents, and even politicians declared that sign language revealed ignorance and that oral methods were far superior to manualists' methods of education. Some deaf students had no other choice but to learn by oralist techniques, but many other deaf community members questioned the oralists' authority, and older community members rebelled against this oppression, empowering their cause with religious rhetoric. Deaf community activists like Veditz disagreed with oralists' arguments and responded with "[a]s long as we have deaf people on earth, we will have signs."[57] Like Veditz, many deaf community members believed their language was a "gift from God" and that God was using Thomas H. Gallaudet to help give deaf Americans that language and through it a way to salvation.

Widow Douglas and Miss Watson encourage Huck to become literate so that he can learn their Protestant theology and know God. While Huck has not claimed to be converted to Protestantism, he shows signs of influence from their kindness. Huck's version of benevolence is evident when he befriends Jim, Miss Watson's slave, who seeks freedom from bondage. Society's values and teachings have physically constrained him. Huck and Jim differ in that Huck is perceived as free, whereas Jim is a slave. Throughout the course of the musical, we see Huck struggling with his relationship to Jim. In breaking the rules of the Protestant society,[58] Huck befriends Jim, a runaway slave. In doing so, he demonstrates his own version of compassion by helping Jim, whom he sees as worse off than himself.

Redemption: Acceptance of Differences and Forgiveness of Self

Part of the Protestant influence in *Big River* is the recognition that all human beings are equal and of worth: We are all "children of God." Huck struggles to reconcile his relationship with Jim and Jim's status as an outsider with regard to Huck's community. Certain scenes in the musical highlight not only Huck's transformation but also the argument that, like the slaves in *Big River*, the members of the American deaf community are equal to members of the hearing community and worthy of recognition as intellectual members of society. While searching for freedom, Jim and Huck find themselves aboard a raft traveling down the Mississippi River. Huck's and Jim's differences are apparent: "Now, with *Big River*, Huck Finn and Jim, the Slave, find themselves being 'worlds apart,' not only in terms of being black and white, but also in terms of being hearing and deaf."[59] Huck is deaf, whereas Jim is hearing. Toward the beginning of act 2, Huck and Jim realize how different they are, yet how strong they are working together. Jim signs and sings, "And I see the same skies through brown eyes / That you see through blue / But we're worlds apart / . . . / Just like the earth, just like the sun / Two worlds together are better than one," and concludes with "[a]nd the mocking bird sings / From the ole yonder tree / Twaddle-ee ah dee dee dum dee dee dee."[60] Huck joins Jim in this song, but as their skin color denotes them as two individuals from two different communities, Jim's ability to hear distinguishes him from Huck as he concludes the song with a reference to the bird he hears singing. Huck does not respond to Jim's last lines because he does not hear the bird; yet, he has understood that Jim is like him in that he is a human being with a perspective all his own.

Big River continues to reinforce the characters' differences—both deaf and hearing and black and white. However, in one critical scene, a gospel-filled song expresses the concept that all humans are equal because they are "children of God." In a funeral scene, the slave Alice sings while both hearing and deaf cast members, who are black and white, join her in signing "How Blest We Are." The song conveys the evangelical theology of redemption through God's son, Jesus, and the demonstration of this redemption through faith in this Redeemer. The slave characters reconcile their captured orientation in this world, and the implication is that the deaf community reconciles its fight to preserve sign language through the belief that God's loving hand controls their experiences. On a candlelit stage the cast signs and sings "How blest we are / As children of a God so good and true / To understand his moving hand / And love for me and you."[61] By staging this song with both hearing and deaf actors signing the song, Deaf West emphasizes the notion that all people are "children of God." The evangelical theology expressed in these lyrics suggests not only that the black slave who is singing the song is as valuable as the white characters standing behind her but also that the deaf characters are equal to the hearing characters. Every character on the stage in this scene signs the song. Since the life experiences of deaf Americans include battles to retain sign language, which is used in this scene to heighten the lyrics' emotional appeal, the ability of sign language to convey deeply religious and emotional sentiments is emphasized.

Also important in this song is the religious metaphor of God's moving hand, which is used to convey the belief that God is in control of believers' life experiences. From a Deaf perspective, God's hand is not only controlling but also symbolic as a conveyor of meaning since sign language expresses meaning on a signer's hands.

As the musical progresses, Huck begins to feel conflicted. Even though Jim is worse off than Huck since he is a slave, he and Huck are sharing a journey to freedom. Huck begins to transform his convictions by questioning slavery, recognizing Jim as his equal and even a father figure. In doing so, he is moving closer to freedom.

Huck's growing acceptance of Jim, an outsider because he is a slave, teaches hearing audiences that, despite differences, everyone should be respected. Members of the deaf community frequently encounter hearing individuals who do not respect deaf values. Historically, sign language was considered not to be a true language, and, by extension, the deaf community itself was believed to be deficient. Deaf Americans have been stereotyped as slow or impaired because of their deafness. For years, and even more recently with the debates on cochlear implants, the deaf community has been subjected to the ignorance of people who view deafness as equivalent to mental or intellectual deficiencies. Historically, this is reflected in oralists' arguments and educational policies. As we have seen, it was through the work of Protestant deaf community leaders that sign language has been secured; through its use in sanctuaries it has been preserved; and in the production of Deaf West's *Big River* its use symbolizes the freedom the deaf community has won from the grips of oralists.

The clearest moment in *Big River*, one that symbolizes the challenges facing the deaf community as its members worked to stabilize and maintain sign language, comes when the young slave girl (who, we learn, is Jim's deaf daughter) signs the spiritual "The Crossing" with her hands in chains while her mother, Alice, sings the following:

> Crossing to the other side
> We are pilgrims
> On a journey through the darkness of the night
> We are bound for other places
> Crossing to the other side
> I will worry 'bout tomorrow
> When tomorrow comes in sight
> Until then, Lord, I'm just a Pilgrim
> Crossing to the other side
> Jesus will be there to meet me
> He will reach his hand in mine
> I will no more be a stranger
> When I reach the other side.[62]

The sight of a deaf character (and actor) signing in chains produces a strong impact (see picture). From a Deaf perspective, the chained hands symbolize the oralists' hold on the deaf community by restricting sign language and promoting the use of speech. With chained hands, movements are restricted, so language and meaning are not easily expressed. However, this deaf actor in *Big River* enriches the production by signing the deeply Protestant lyrics sung by the hearing actress portraying her mother.

Visually expressing the strife experienced by the American deaf community, Deaf West employs a dramatic staging convention to relate the oralists' stronghold on deaf people in the first half of the twentieth century. The result is that *Big River* is a work that raises the awareness of the audience, who may gain an appreciation for sign language and its ability to convey meaning for deaf people. Deaf West's *Big River* may even encourage audience members to accept the differences they may have with deaf people and become advocates of Deaf culture by attending more

Left to right: Alice (Gwen Stewart) and Alice's daughter (Michelle A. Banks).[63]

productions by Deaf West Theatre, supporting captioning at their local movie theater, or sharing with their friends what they experienced at *Big River*. As audiences spread the word that the deaf community has achieved a masterful performance that is both enlightening and entertaining, the mission of both Deaf West and the early deaf activists is fulfilled. The religious rhetoric in this case of the deaf slave girl imparts strength to her character—she finds power in a belief that is greater than the society that is keeping her in chains.

The spiritual "The Crossing" is an example of how religious themes in *Big River* intertwine with the mission of Deaf West. As a deaf girl, the young slave signs about finding a better place beyond this world. She passionately conveys the act of "crossing to another side" with the sign implying going from one place to another. Because the sign is executed at a location higher than typical, the meaning signified is "crossing to heaven." In Twain's original work, slaves are clearly portrayed as outsiders of the Protestant American community in which they live. In Deaf West's *Big River*, deaf Americans play the role of outsiders as well. "The Crossing" poignantly points to the hope that both groups of outsiders may have found in their religious faiths: that something better lies beyond this earth. This belief is common in American evangelical Protestantism, which holds that "Jesus Christ (crucified—dead—resurrected) [is] God's means of redemption."[64] In *Big River*, as Alice sings and her daughter signs "Jesus will be there to meet me / He will reach his hand in mine,"[65] one is reminded of not only evangelical Protestant theology but also the importance of hands to the deaf community. As a community that identifies itself by a visual language that is conveyed on the hands, body, and face of the signer, it is Jesus's hand that will touch the deaf slave girl when she reaches heaven—the ultimate redeemer in Protestant theology. The song continues with "I will no more be a stranger,"[66] referring to the outsider status assigned to both slaves and deaf Americans. The song this deaf slave girl signs implies that through salvation freedom is found in death, when she will no longer be a slave. For many deaf Americans, freedom was won when new laws and policies—as fought for by deaf activists—acknowledged their value and granted them more rights.

Before Huck can gain personal freedom, he must experience redemption. Although both Huck and Jim are on a river that is taking them to freedom, physically for Jim and personally for Huck, they are seeking redemption for different reasons. In *Big River*, as in Twain's *Adventures of Huckleberry Finn*, the audience learns that Jim has a deaf daughter, as mentioned earlier. For *Big River* audiences this may explain why Jim knows sign language and is able to communicate with Huck. Jim voices and signs the story of when he learned his daughter was deaf:

> Before I could hit her again, 'long come the wind and slam the door to, blam! And my Lord, *the child never move*. My breath hopped right out

> of me. Oh, Huck! I burst out cryin' and grab her. Lord God Almighty forgive Jim, I says, 'cause he ain't never going to forgive himself as long as he live! That fever left her deaf and dumb, Huck. Plumb deaf and dumb. And I'd been treating her so.[67]

In telling this story, Jim shares his need for redemption—he had mistreated his daughter without realizing there was an explanation for her not following his instructions. Jim makes it clear that his guilt is insurmountable, yet he asks for God's forgiveness. Jim demonstrates the Protestant belief that God's grace redeems him. Jim also shows his trust in Huck by sharing this story and demonstrates that it is through the shared language of signs that they can connect—one hearing, one deaf, and one searching for physical freedom, one searching for personal freedom.

Huck's road to redemption is challenging and complicated. When Jim first tells Huck of his plans to buy his wife and children, Huck reacts with conflicting emotions. Facing the audience, Huck signs, "Then my conscience got to troubling me. This thing I was doing was coming home. Thinks I: Jim's going to get free. . . . And who's to blame for it? Me. . . . My conscience was stirring me up, hotter than ever."[68] Huck feels conflicted by the Protestant beliefs ingrained in him by the Widow Douglas and Miss Watson. Helping Jim steal another person's "property" would surely send him down the path of damnation. But Huck's instinct is to help Jim; Huck believes it isn't right that the society he lives in would support separating a man from his family and make women and men property.

Huck decides to do wrong by doing right. He signs to the audience, "What's the use in learning to do right when it's troublesome to do right and no trouble to do wrong, and the wages is just the same?"[69] Huck helps Jim but struggles with the desire to do what is right by the Protestant standards of the Widow Douglas and Miss Watson. In the end he decides that going to hell and feeling like hell would be the results of either decision—to help Jim or not to help him. Jim is captured by a family down river, and Huck once again debates what to do. Huck turns to the audience and signs, "Human beings can be so cruel to each other. It hit me all of a sudden that here was the hand of God, letting me know I'd been watched all along from above . . . I decided to pray and see if I could stop being the kind of boy I was. But you can't pray a lie."[70] Huck believes God is watching him and will punish him for his decision to go against the Protestant ethics of his society. He decides to work through his admission by writing a letter to Miss Watson. Huck confesses his sin; he feels redeemed—"washed clean of sin."[71] However, in the next second he tears up the letter because of the relationship he has established with Jim. Huck's true redemption is not through Protestant salvation but through his decision to be true to himself and his own beliefs. He chooses what is right for him and Jim as outsiders rather than following the entrenched assumptions of their society. The deaf community has a history of others, typically hearing people, making decisions for them that affect their education, their worship, and their entertainment. Once the deaf community had empowered itself and publicly claimed that its members are advocates for themselves and their language—through the NAD films, the DPN protest, and artful expression like theater productions—it repositioned itself within the hearing world. This new position challenged limited assumptions about people who are deaf and their abilities to work, think, and communicate.

Freedom: The Shining Light

Huck comes to symbolize the struggles the deaf community must have encountered with a growing oralist movement that saw deaf people as separate from the rest of the hearing world. In *Big River*, Deaf West Theatre exploits the differences of Jim and Huck to advocate for full inclusion—two different cultures working together. In doing so, those at Deaf West Theatre become deaf activists, vigilantly advocating the recognition of a deaf identity that includes the struggle to use and preserve sign language. In "Worlds Apart" Huck and Jim sign and sing that "[t]wo worlds together are better than one."[72] In *Big River*, Deaf West Theatre has chosen to symbolize this with the use of a spoken and signed performance. The bicultural experience combining the two worlds of hearing and deaf people makes for a compelling theater experience while adding significance to the themes of *Big River*, based on Twain's *Adventures of Huckleberry Finn*.

As Huck and Jim travel down the Mississippi River, they both encounter challenges that change them, yet they both find freedom. Huck questions the societal and political beliefs that gave rise to slavery. As mentioned earlier, he begins to see Jim as a friend or even a father figure. Huck feels no loyalty to the rules of the church and the state and begins to follow his heart; in doing so he obtains a personal freedom. He helps Jim escape even if it means he will go to hell. However, through the wishes of Miss Watson, Jim is granted his physical freedom. Huck recognizes that he has believed what he has been told to believe and that he has done little thinking for himself. Reflecting on his confusion, Huck signs the following:

> I have lived in the darkness for so long
> I am waitin' for the light to shine
> Far beyond horizons I have seen
> Beyond the things I've been
> Beyond the dreams I've dreamed
> Are the things I've done
> In fact each and every one
> Are [*sic*] the way that I was taught to run
> I am waitin' for the light to shine!
> I am waitin' for the light to shine
> I have lived in the darkness for so long
> I'm waitin' for the light to shine.[73]

For Huck, the light may be the ideas and beliefs that he develops on his own, independently of those of society. For the deaf community, these lyrics have far greater significance.

Toward the end of *Big River*, Huck, Alice, Alice's daughter, Jim, and the company take the stage and sing and sign "Waitin' for the Light to Shine." At one point in the performance of the song, the singers stop singing and the instruments stop playing. The stage is filled with deaf and hearing actors signing the lyrics in silence—"I have lived in the darkness for so long / I'm waitin' for the light to shine"[74]—hands dancing in rhythm, conveying a message in unison. The audience is reminded of the bicultural experience they are having and of the significance of a deaf-hearing theater event. The deaf members of the audience fully understand what is being expressed, but I argue that Deaf West's decision to perform this song this way is a political one. Deaf West makes the hearing audience "deaf" if only for the duration of this song. Hearing audience members sit in silence, watching sign language convey a meaning that many of them do not understand. This moment allows them a slight glimpse into the deaf community and the deaf identity, both of which value the use of sign language. The lyrics have many interpretations when examined from a Deaf perspective. The deaf community was once kept in the dark in the sense of its right to education, to marriage, and even to its own language. When analyzing these lyrics in the context of this struggle, many important topics emerge. The importance of light for deaf people is literal: Since sign language is a visual language, light is needed so that signs can be seen and understood. Another interpretation is based on the Protestant themes evident in the lyrics when considered in the context of the American deaf community's history of the intertwining of education, sign language advocacy, and religion.

Historically, deaf Americans were referred to as living in darkness when they were without language and religion. As mentioned in chapter 1, in his opening address at the American School for the Deaf, Thomas H. Gallaudet used the metaphor of darkness and light. He referred to deaf people as imprisoned in dungeons, thus in darkness.[75] He preached that sign language would light deaf persons' paths to understanding and knowledge of the

Protestant faith. In *Big River*, Huck is struggling with what path to take. He has been taught that there are only two to choose from: the path of salvation, taught to him by Miss Watson, and the path of damnation, demonstrated to him by his pap. Pap symbolizes the darkness of society, whereas the light Huck needs to make his decision is already within him.

Jim and Huck work together throughout their adventure. They gain respect for and learn to trust each other. They go against the norms of their separate societies and accept one another. As hearing and deaf actor together convey through sign language and spoken English their characters' emotions and the musical's bicultural emphasis, they symbolically float on a river of mainstreaming, advocating the use of sign language and recognizing its value. They blend speaking and singing with signing to reach both deaf and hearing audiences. During "Muddy Water" the two actors collaborate to create signs (see picture). While riding their raft down the river, Huck and Jim—one deaf and one hearing—rely on each other for safety, for camaraderie, and for the conveyance of meaning. Huck learns that, like the Mississippi, he must continue to move forward by learning from and trusting in friends and that freedom does not come in isolation. He gains redemption by trusting his conscience, not the ingrained assumptions of society.

For deaf Americans, the value of a community bonded by a common language is significant. Deaf West Theatre has created a production that advocates for the use and recognition of sign language. In doing so, it uses religious subject matter rhetorically to convince audiences of the value of sign language and the merging of both deaf and hearing cultures. While both speaking and sign language are used in Deaf West's *Big River*, the audience witnesses a clear and graceful art form empowering the American deaf community, whose respect for sign language echoes the early manualists' claim that it is "a gift from God" and should be valued.

Jim (Rufus Bonds Jr.) and Huck (Tyrone Giordano) creating a sign together.[76]

As audience members, we learn that we need to rethink many of our society's assumptions—from our ideas of theater to our preconceptions of the deaf community. Deaf West's production of *Big River* is a simple story of one boy's voyage of spiritual awakening; however, with the added context of the deaf community's struggles, the production is also a significant achievement of advocacy for the deaf community. Audiences observe the ability of the deaf community members—from Jim's deaf slave daughter signing in chains to a deaf lead actor—to use sign language effectively to command the attention of an audience of both deaf and hearing people hanging on every sign.

Conclusion

The message of Deaf West Theatre's production of *Big River* echoes the early motives of Veditz and the Gallaudets. In 1817, Gallaudet opened the first school for the deaf in America. The main principle of the school was to give the deaf a language so they could gain understanding of religion. The story in *Big River* takes place in 1840. By this time, several schools for the deaf had opened in America promoting sign language as the means and skill needed for the deaf to learn. However, by the latter half of the nineteenth century, deaf people found their language under attack by educators who believed it was primitive and showed ignorance; thus the need for the NAD films promoting and preserving sign language. Because Deaf West's production uses deaf and hearing actors who sign and sing to tell the story, the production is a symbol to the deaf and hearing audience of how far the deaf community has come—from a defensive position to an offensive one promoting the artistic expressions of the community. It is also a reflection of a deaf identity ingrained with the evangelical Protestant ethic to serve the greater good of the community by educating others of its struggles to preserve sign language and gain recognition and respect for it.

Like their fellow advocates of the past, the NAD continues to use contemporary and effective means necessary to persuade both deaf and hearing audiences of their cause. The NAD is the "largest constituency organization safeguarding the accessibility and civil rights of 28 million deaf and hard of hearing Americans in education, employment, health care, and telecommunications."[77] As activism within the deaf community takes different forms, one constant will continue to connect the community to Protestantism: the inherent link of the advocacy for sign language with religious rhetoric to preserve it.

Notes

1. Schirmer, *Psychological, Social, and Educational Dimensions to Deafness*, 93.
2. Ibid.
3. Jankowski, *Deaf Empowerment*, 28.
4. Burch, *Signs of Resistance*, 57.
5. Master signers are deaf or hearing members of the deaf community who are highly skilled in the use of sign language.
6. Fernandes and Kelleher, "Signs of Eloquence," 182.
7. Ibid.
8. Baynton, Gannon, and Bergey, *Through Deaf Eyes*, 109.
9. Ibid.
10. Van Cleve and Crouch, *Place of Their Own*, 141.
11. Ibid., 74.
12. Burch, *Signs of Resistance*, 58.
13. Ibid.
14. Jankowski, *Deaf Empowerment*, 61; Burch, *Signs of Resistance*, 52; Padden, "Translating Veditz," 251.
15. Burch, *Signs of Resistance*, 57–58.
16. Van Cleve and Crouch, *Place of Their Own*, 141.
17. Burch, *Signs of Resistance*, 58.
18. Ibid., 59.
19. Nineteenth-century oralists were influenced by Darwin's theory of evolution and viewed deaf people as less evolved and sign language as akin to the gestures of animals.
20. NAD has made the film available through YouTube at http://youtu.be/XITbj3NTLUQ.
21. Padden, "Translating Veditz," 251.
22. Veditz, *Preservation of the Sign Language*.
23. Padden, "Translating Veditz," 247.
24. Veditz, *Preservation of the Sign Language*.
25. Ibid.
26. Gannon, *Deaf Heritage*, 193.

27. Ibid.

28. The blog *Deaf Ministries Connection*, at http://deafministries-connection.wordpress.com/, lists Deaf churches and interpreted services throughout the United States. It also lists international deaf ministries. This information has been collected since 1995.

29. This was attempted by Emerson Romero, a deaf man from New York. See Strauss, *New Civil Right*, 205; Gannon, *Deaf Heritage*, 266.

30. Strauss, *New Civil Right*, 205.

31. Baynton, Gannon, and Bergey, *Through Deaf Eyes*, 123.

32. Strauss, *New Civil Right*, 211.

33. Ibid., 230.

34. Ibid., 236.

35. For more information on the details of the Deaf President Now protest, see Christiansen and Barnartt, *Deaf President Now!*

36. Gannon, *Week the World Heard Gallaudet*, 15.

37. Ibid., 87.

38. Ibid., 113.

39. Bove is best known for her work on *Sesame Street*.

40. Deaf here is capitalized to signify these individuals' physical deafness as well as their cultural identification with the Deaf culture.

41. Waterstreet, quoted in Performing for Los Angeles Youth, *Teacher's Guide*, 1.

42. Waterstreet, quoted in Garfield, "Deaf West Theatre," 15.

43. Winship, "*Big River* Signed, Sung on Broadway."

44. Calhoun, quoted in Performing for Los Angeles Youth, *Student Guide/Discovery Journal*, 15.

45. O'Brien, quoted in ibid., 14.

46. Cohen, "Big River," 56.

47. See Buechner, *Speak What We Feel*; Holland, "Soul-Butter and Hogwash"; Sattelmeyer and Crowley, *One Hundred Years of* Huckleberry Finn; Hays, "Mark Twain's Rebellion against God."

48. See Brodwin, "Mark Twain in the Pulpit"; Hays, "Mark Twain's Rebellion against God"; Holland, "Soul-Butter and Hogwash."

49. Brodwin, "Mark Twain in the Pulpit," 371.

50. A term Stanley Brodwin used to refer to the transformation of Christian principles made by Twain. Emphasis in original.

51. Twain, quoted in Brodwin, "Mark Twain in the Pulpit," 371.

52. Brodwin, "Mark Twain in the Pulpit," 385.

53. Padden, "People of the Eye," 10.

54. In *Adventures of Huckleberry Finn*, the reader learns from Jim, the slave, that his daughter is deaf. Jim tells Huck the emotional story of when he first learned that his daughter was deaf.

55. "Do Ya Wanna Go to Heaven?" soundtrack.

56. Ibid.

57 Veditz, *Preservation of the Sign Language.*

58. See Mark A. Noll's chapter, "The Bible and Slavery," in *America's God,* for a discussion of how American Protestants of the nineteenth century used Bible passages to argue both for slavery and against slavery and to present arguments mediating between the two extremes.

59. Garfield, "Deaf West Theatre," 15.

60. "Worlds Apart" soundtrack.

61. "How Blest We Are" soundtrack.

62. "The Crossing" soundtrack.

63. Performing for Los Angeles Youth, *Student Guide/Discovery Journal,* 8. Photo by Craig Schwartz. Courtesy Deaf West Theatre.

64. Noll, *America's God,* 171.

65. "The Crossing" soundtrack.

66. Ibid.

67. Hauptman, *Big River,* 77.

68. Ibid., 51.

69. Ibid., 53.

70. Ibid., 94.

71. Ibid.

72. "Worlds Apart" soundtrack.

73. "Waitin' for the Light to Shine," in soundtrack to *Big River: The Adventures of Huckleberry Finn.*

74. Ibid.

75. Gallaudet, "Sermon Delivered at the Opening," 8.

76. Performing for Los Angeles Youth, *Student Guide/Discovery Journal,* 9. "About NAD." Photo by Craig Schwartz. Courtesy Deaf West Theatre.

5 Conclusion and Implications

IN THE nineteenth and early twentieth centuries, Deaf advocacy for sign language in the United States was grounded in religious discourse. As Thomas H. Gallaudet brought education to deaf people in the United States with the opening of the American School for the Deaf in 1817, he more profoundly brought Protestant religion as well, and that influence would leave an imprint on the American deaf identity. As chapter 1 explains, Gallaudet's efforts to bring education and language to deaf people stemmed from his conviction that it was his mission to help others to know God. This Protestant influence on deaf education left a lasting impression on the deaf community, which emerged because residential schools brought together deaf individuals who had been living apart. As more schools for deaf children emerged in the latter half of the nineteenth century, oralists supported a national identity that emphasized the importance of speaking a common language. Because deaf individuals did not speak, they were set apart as outsiders in their own country. Fueling this state of affairs was the growing support for the oral tradition of education. As science progressed and influenced popular thinking, oralists used theories of evolution and eugenics to back up their claims that deaf persons needed to learn to speak and lipread in order to be on equal status with hearing Americans. For *pure* oralists, the use of sign language was evidence of a lower stage of evolution.

The religious rhetoric found in schools, sanctuaries, and the American deaf community's social activism engendered a deaf identity that proved crucial in confronting challenges posed by a dominant hearing community that threatened to end the use of sign language. The nineteenth- and early twentieth-century arguments favoring the use of manualism or the combined method of instruction (the latter was the chosen method of deaf ministers to convey sermons in signs and to advocate for the political interests of the emerging community) and the efforts to garner support for deaf community advocacy have cemented a deaf identity grounded in the use of sign language. Although society at large has become more secular while participation in religious services and evidence of religion's presence in the deaf community have perhaps diminished since the last half of the twentieth century, I argue that the Protestant religion is still tied to the deaf community through the use of sign language.

As the previous chapters illustrate, deaf Americans have faced challenges specific to their language use. By emphasizing speech and lipreading, oralists threatened the existence of sign language in schools for deaf children. In response, the deaf community united to defend its claim to sign language. Late nineteenth-century debates on deaf education often split along ideological lines. Manualists aligned their arguments in favor of sign language with a Protestant ideology that endorsed the bringing of sign language to deaf Americans. Many viewed sign language as the "natural language of deaf people"—a theory that is supported by Gary Morgan's and Judy Kegl's study of Nicaraguan sign language among deaf children in two different schools.[1] The combined system of educating deaf students was supported by many deaf community leaders. This method valorized both oral and manual teaching, emphasizing thereby that all deaf students should learn sign language and that sign language would be the method of communication in all matters of religious training and instruction. Oralists, influenced by advancements in science, cited evolutionary theories to support the view that sign language use was characteristic of a species of lower development. Deaf individuals were outsiders to the hearing community, which was struggling to define its national identity, as well as to Christian educators who were seeking to save the heathens. In these challenging times, the deaf community appealed to the like-minded Protestant hearing community, using their shared religious beliefs as a way to build bridges and garner support for sign language.

In addition to the dormitories and the vocational classes, the chapel typically remained a signing place at residential schools. Religious training maintained its importance at deaf residential schools well into the twentieth century. Chapel services not only transmitted the deaf community's recognition of the value of sign language but also perpetuated a deaf identity that exuded morality. As oralists and manualists split on how to educate deaf students, they often agreed that religious training should be carried out in sign language. The reasons for this, as I explain in chapter 3, were grounded in physical practicality and in the capability of sign language to best convey the abstract theology of a sermon. Sign language could effectively convey the religious rhetoric to a deaf audience, whereas spoken English could not.

While sign language continued to be transmitted in the chapel, religious services also had the effect of connecting young deaf students with a larger deaf community. Deaf ministers who came to schools to deliver sermons were often the only deaf role models for deaf students in the mid-nineteenth and early twentieth centuries. When students graduated from the residential schools, they sought social interaction at churches, where they knew they would find other signing deaf individuals. The Protestant church thus served as a signing sanctuary for the deaf community. Deaf leaders emerged from ministries to deaf people, and the pulpit became a platform for not just religious training but also an expression of community values. The political interests of the deaf community were often supported by the church, and the church became a location where strong bonds were formed among deaf people. In these ways the Protestant church played a major role in the deaf community by maintaining a deaf identity most recognizable by the use of sign language.

As the deaf community faced continuing struggles, its members were often defensive in their responses to the dominant hearing community. Turning to artful expressions and modern technology, the deaf community fought to preserve sign language. Historically the deaf community preserved master signers on film, and George W. Veditz's leadership gave rise to the NAD's moving picture campaign. Veditz's *Preservation of the Sign Language* is legendary in the deaf community. His fiery biblical metaphors characterize oralists as the new pharaohs who are coming to enslave the signing deaf community. Veditz's powerful ethos greatly influenced the deaf community, and his pathos appealed to a still mainly Protestant nation in the early twentieth century.

As deaf activism evolved throughout the twentieth century, it took many forms, the most profound of which was the Deaf President Now protest in 1988. Using the liberatory rhetoric of the civil rights movement before it, the DPN protest included students, faculty, staff, and other deaf community advocates, who successfully persuaded the Gallaudet University board of directors to elect the institution's first Deaf president. The DPN movement was seen and heard on television by many people around the world. This protest was one of the factors that influenced the passage of the Americans with Disabilities Act in 1990.

Deaf activism and advocacy have been located in many places and relevant to many areas of deaf people's lives—including telecommunication through TTYs and TDDs and access to entertainment and information through captions. What has emerged is what I claim is a Deaf rhetoric that will forever maintain features of the heavy Protestant influence established at the inception of the first American school for deaf people in 1817.

Deaf rhetoric is evident in the early arguments to preserve sign language and the twenty-first-century contentions for its recognition and value. We see this most effectively in another location and artful expression of deaf activism: the Deaf West Theatre's production of *Big River: The Adventures of Huckleberry Finn*. This production reached thousands of people on its national tour and is an example of a shift in Deaf activism from a defensive stance to an offensive one. In this musical, with its religious themes and references, contemporary leaders in the deaf community cause both deaf and hearing audiences to reflect on the use of sign language and the treatment of deaf people in the United States. This one secular example of deaf activism exhibits a link to Protestant religion, suggesting that the religious imprint on the American deaf identity continues even today; thus, Deaf rhetoric that includes Protestant features is an effective use of sign language in Deaf advocacy with any audience—hearing or deaf.

We are now left asking about the implications of this Protestant influence on an American deaf identity. I contend that significant evidence suggests that more research is needed on rhetoric, writing studies, deaf studies, and disability studies.

Historically, the church played a role in shaping a deaf identity; however, is this still the case today? Even though a number of members of the American deaf community are presently active participants in deaf and hearing congregations, the church's role as a social and political place for them may not be as vital as it was in the past, when the church served as a site in which deaf people could socialize. Advancements in technology now allow deaf people to interact without meeting in person and also provides platforms for deaf activism, much as the church did in the early twentieth century. For example, the Internet has become an active place for Deaf advocacy, as evidenced by the NAD's presence on YouTube and Facebook (several other deaf advocacy groups also utilize Facebook). As technology has provided the deaf community greater access to the world, it also has implications for a deaf identity and the community's cohesion.

Implications of Technology: Coalescing or Fragmenting a Deaf Identity?

Technology unquestionably plays an important role in the deaf community. It has not always been used to unite the community, however. Historically, certain technological developments brought about another way in which the deaf community was set apart from the hearing community. For example, in 1876 Alexander Graham Bell, prominent oralist and opponent of sign language, demonstrated his voice telephone at the Centennial Exhibition in Philadelphia. Bell's invention further separated deaf from hearing people at a pivotal time in the history of the deaf community. Because the successful use of the telephone relied on users' ability to speak and hear, deaf people were excluded. It was not until 1964 that the first teletypewriters (TTY) were introduced; with TTYs, deaf individuals were able to communicate over phone lines.

When films were first introduced, they were all silent, and both deaf and hearing audiences could enjoy the new medium together. In fact, deaf actors were used in some silent films. When sound was added to motion pictures, deaf audiences were excluded. Although captions were added to films for the benefit of deaf audiences, they were not widely used until much later in the twentieth century. Technological advancements have played an interesting role in the deaf community. Certain developments have caused the deaf community to unite in its activism.

The benefits of technology cannot be overstated; however, in the case of the American deaf community, a critical look at the negative aspects of technology is appropriate. Do members of the deaf community have equal access to telecommunication technologies? As Bell's telephone invention brought ease of communication to the hearing community, so the TTY and computer technology have brought distant deaf community members together without requiring face-to-face, in-person contact. The TDD and video relay service (VRS) have become accessible to a wide swath of the deaf community. Only recently has more sophisticated technology become available at affordable rates to deaf people. In the twenty-first century, VRS can be used on mobile devices using 3G technology. Since 3G service is fairly common, many individuals can access VRS. Telecommunication technology has finally made it possible for deaf people to use sign language to communicate via telephone lines or Internet connections rather than having to type.

Communication for deaf community members can occur from anywhere and does not require them to meet in person, and those who have greater access to more sophisticated technology may be further separated from those who have less or no access to such technology. While there are deaf individuals at every social level just as hearing individuals, the access to sophisticated technology may be restricted to those who can afford it. Mobile devices (cell phones and tablets) are fairly affordable with data plans that can access 3G technology and Wi-Fi. With these mobile devices, deaf people can communicate through text messages and VRS, but we have no statistical information on how many deaf people own and use such devices. More study on how the deaf community uses technology would be interesting and reveal whether technology is acting as a coalescing agent for a national deaf community.

Of course, technology has also helped deaf people gain broader access to information. Although captioning has enabled deaf people to get their news from television or enjoy the same shows as their hearing friends and family members, it was slow to occur. In the 1990s a federal law was passed to phase in captioning for all television shows. Deaf people who want to see a captioned film must do some research to find a local theater that provides such opportunities. Websites like Captionfish help locate theaters and show times for captioned films. Most theaters offer CaptiView, a portable technology that fits in the drink holder of the movie viewer's seat. A flexible arm with a screen on it can be positioned in front of the viewer to enable the person to read the captions and watch the film. This technology allows equal movie-viewing opportunities for deaf and hearing audiences.

Although technology provides greater access to mainstream America for some deaf and hard of hearing individuals, it has also divided the community by raising the question of what it means to be Deaf/deaf. To discuss technology and its implications for uniting or dividing the deaf community, I must briefly examine cochlear implants. Many parents of deaf children view cochlear implants as miraculous inventions that allow their children a permanent place in the mainstream. With greater use of these devices in the 1990s came protests by the deaf community, claiming that cochlear implants threatened the existence of the Deaf culture.

Technology has given hard of hearing people better hearing devices and led to the sophistication of cochlear implants, which scientists and doctors have worked to perfect since the mid-twentieth century. A cochlear implant is a prosthetic replacement for the inner ear (cochlea). When sound is converted into electrical impulses by the external parts of the device, the small implanted wires touching the cochlea stimulate the hearing nerve. A cochlear implant does not restore natural hearing and does not act like a hearing aid, which amplifies sounds. A person with a cochlear implant works to decipher the electrical pulses as language.

In the 1990s I attended a DeafNation Expo in California, where an artwork display addressed the subject of cochlear implants. Many of the drawings and paintings were interpretations of mutilations of ears graphically portraying the spilled blood resulting from implants. At that time, many deaf community members, like these artists, argued that implants were physically dangerous and posed a threat to Deaf culture.[2] Today these arguments have died down somewhat. Evidence of this is the change in the sign for "cochlear implant." In the 1990s, "cochlear implant" was signed with the sign for "vampire" placed behind the ear on the signer's head, signifying the deaf community's contempt for the device. Today a more frequent and politically correct sign for cochlear implant is simply C-I. This change reflects a difference in attitude that also suggests a wider acceptance by the deaf community of not only implants but possibly people with cochlear implants as well. Many parents who have obtained cochlear implants for their children take NAD's suggestion seriously and have their child learn both spoken English and sign language. By practicing sign language, more people with cochlear implants will participate in the deaf community, which has likely led to the latter's greater acceptance of these people. The "NAD Position on Cochlear Implants" implores parents of children who are deaf that "[t]hroughout the developmental years, the deaf child—implanted or not, mainstreamed or not—should receive education in deaf studies, including deaf heritage, history of deafness and deaf people, particularly stories and accounts of deaf people who have succeeded in many areas of life."[3]

The advent of technology means that deaf individuals no longer need to be face to face in order to communicate; now they can take advantage of instant messaging, real-time chat, TDD, and videophones. Although the NAD reports that deaf Americans typically earn lower wages than most hearing Americans, technology has become more affordable; yet, certain technological developments are still out of reach for some deaf people. With more and more people using these new forms of communication, bridges have been formed between deaf communities all over the world and between deaf and hearing peers. For example, I have developed online relationships with deaf educators at Gallaudet University and friends in other states. Free video applications such as Skype and Tango have allowed me to hold conversations in sign language with people who do not live near me.

Just as technology has affected the social relationships of hearing individuals, it has also had a small impact on the lives of deaf people. Where the sanctuary once served a significant social function in a deaf individual's life, technology now allows that socializing to occur in the comfort of one's own home. Once the pulpit was used to further political interests of deaf people; now the presence of the NAD has become overwhelming both online and in lobbying efforts in Washington, DC. The NAD has been key in securing captioning for the deaf community and ensuring technological updates in federal offices that anticipate the needs of deaf and hard of hearing employees and customers.[4] The organization's use of technology and the Internet continues the earlier work of the church and church leaders. Technology has played a significant role in shaping and projecting a deaf identity.

Implications for Future Scholarship

As rhetoricians we uncover aspects of the communities we investigate. I have uncovered the use of religious rhetoric by the Deaf community in the United States to advocate for the preservation of sign language. While I was conducting research for this study, it struck me that this community has emerged on U.S. soil and is identified by its language use; yet, very little is written about it in the field of rhetoric. Gallaudet University's archives are full of interesting rhetorical documents that are ripe for analysis. Speeches and sermons by deaf ministers, educators, and deaf community leaders are preserved on film and in papers. The Gallaudet University library also houses a large collection of periodicals specific to the deaf community; these journals contain articles and other information that may interest rhetoricians. Because rhetoric scholars often neglect the religious aspect of their subject matter, whether it appears in people or in texts, it is possible the deaf community's rhetoric has long been overlooked because of its overwhelmingly Protestant component.

It is important that our research recognizes the large role played by religion and spiritual matters in people's experiences in general and how that role comes to light in their rhetoric. As Beth Daniell states, "When whole areas of people's lives are closed off as unworthy of academic attention, the academy misses important information."[5] Protestantism has played such a significant role in the evolution of the American deaf community that to overlook it would be a serious omission. Furthermore, while many of the deaf community's historical documents project a strong religious deaf identity, research on other aspects of the community's use of language, such as delivery and charisma, would benefit the field of rhetoric as well. Since the rhetor's body is used to convey meaning in Deaf rhetoric, delivery needs to be understood as imparting more than inflection, intonation, and gesture. All of these features are used in signing through body posturing, facial expression, and hand movement. Because of these aspects of the language, hearing people are often moved by sign interpretations of speakers or performances. After interpreting speaking or musical performances, I have been told by hearing audience members that something they have heard before made more sense to them seeing it signed. This element of sign language is charisma.

To recognize a Deaf rhetoric is to recognize an element of a deaf identity that is often overlooked in research with college students. As more and more deaf students attend predominantly hearing postsecondary institutions, it becomes more important for writing studies to consider the identity of deaf students in the classroom. By investigating the experiences of contemporary deaf students in composition classes, we can devise ways to best teach all students. I suggest that qualitative studies,[6] including ethnographies, should be conducted on learning situations that include both deaf and hearing students. Specifically, studies should be carried out on writing classes that include deaf, hard of hearing, and hearing students. How the instructor disseminates information to all students with the assistance of sign language interpreters and how that information is received are significant factors that inform the instructor's formation of strategies to better teach a diverse population of students. Because students have different learning aptitudes, presenting information and assignments in different forms, orally and visually, for example, is one way of helping deaf and hard of hearing students as well as students with auditory processing disorders. Using the basic approaches of Universal Design for Learning would best serve all of the students in a classroom.[7] In addition, deaf students who attend predominantly hearing postsecondary institutions may be straddling deaf and hearing identities. Investigations that uncover the role a student's deaf identity plays in the student's academic identity would be valuable to both writing studies and deaf studies.

Many works in American deaf studies mention Thomas H. Gallaudet's religious affiliation. Although my research has examined the strong Protestant influence in the history of deaf education and the deaf community in the United States through ministries by Protestant churches through the twentieth century, very little if any work has been done on contemporary influences. Many churches provide support to the deaf community through interpreted services, sign language classes, and deaf ministries. Some of these ministries are quite elaborate and include advocacy work for the deaf community. One Baptist church in south Florida where I volunteered offered an afterschool program for deaf children and a once-a-week evening class for parents of deaf children. Since the majority of deaf children are born to hearing parents, this evening class was helpful in supporting the parents, who were learning sign language, acquiring video relay for their children to use, and navigating the public school system. The afterschool program supported mainstreamed deaf children by helping with homework and providing a social space for them to be together. Like residential schools of the past, this afterschool program emphasized moral behavior and included biblical teachings with enjoyable activities. In addition, this particular church provided a separate Bible study class for deaf adults and at one time had four different interpreters volunteering to make services and events inclusive for both deaf and hearing congregants.

Ethnographic work should be done with deaf adults who maintain strong religious aspects of their identity and examine how these relate to their preferred language use. Questions that may be asked include, what role is the church playing in advocacy for the deaf community? Deaf churches and ministries still serve a large population of deaf Americans, but with more secularization in U.S. society at large, has this aspect of a deaf identity stratified and fragmented the deaf community? Traditionally, deaf people do not earn as much money as hearing people; how does this affect the success of a Deaf church? Churches have used technology to minister to deaf people. The Omega Project, founded by Deaf Missions, set out to make available to deaf people the entire Bible in ASL. So far, the New Testament and several books of the Old Testament have been completed and are available on DVD, a mobile application, and MPEG-4 files.[8] With advancements in mobile technology, I am left asking what impact will technology have on worship choices made by deaf people?

Another area that is tied to the role of the church in the current deaf community is the mission work to deaf people, which has existed since Thomas H. Gallaudet's day. Specifically, international work has been a major part of this mission work. Many organizations have emerged that serve deaf people around the world. For example, Deaf Opportunity OutReach (DOOR) International is a nondenominational Christian organization of predominantly deaf people who are working to reach deaf people all over the world and share "the good news of Jesus Christ."[9] A subsidiary of DOOR International is Sasa Designs by the Deaf, which provides deaf artisans in Kenya with employment and fair wages. This international component of deaf activism employs Deaf rhetoric:

"Creating opportunities for the Deaf through this business is a tangible expression of God's love for them."[10] I argue that more work needs to be done exploring international deaf communities and the role religion has played in shaping them.

Notes

1. See Morgan and Kegl, "Nicaraguan Sign Language and Theory of Mind: The Issue of Critical Periods and Abilities."
2. For more information on debates surrounding cochlear implants, see the documentary *Sound and Fury*.
3. "NAD Position Statement on Cochlear Implants."
4. National Association of the Deaf.
5. Daniell, *Communion of Friendship*, 150.
6. See, for example, the study in Babcock, *Tell Me How It Reads*.
7. See the CAST website for more information on the principles of Universal Design for Learning.
8. See Deaf Missions website.
9. See DOOR International website.
10. See Sasa Designs by the Deaf website.

Bibliography

Armstrong, David F. *Original Signs: Gesture, Sign, and the Sources of Language.* Washington, DC: Gallaudet University Press, 1999.

Averitt, Ed. *ASDB 75th Commemoration: 1912–1989.* Arizona Schools for the Deaf and Blind, 1989.

Babcock, Rebecca Day. *Tell Me How It Reads: Tutoring Deaf and Hearing Students in the Writing Center.* Washington, DC: Gallaudet University Press, 2012.

Baynton, Douglas C. *Forbidden Signs: American Culture and the Campaign against Sign Language.* Chicago: University of Chicago Press, 1996.

———. "'Savages and Deaf-Mutes': Evolutionary Theory and the Campaign against Sign Language in the Nineteenth Century." In *Deaf History Unveiled: Interpretations from the New Scholarship,* edited by John Vickrey Van Cleve, 92–112. Washington: Gallaudet University Press, 1993.

———, J. R. Gannon, and J. L. Bergey. *Through Deaf Eyes: A Photographic History of an American Community.* Washington, DC: Gallaudet University Press, 2007.

Benderly, Beryl Lieff. *Dancing without Music: Deafness in America.* New York: Anchor Press/Doubleday, 1980.

Berg, Otto B. and Henry L. Buzzard. *Thomas Gallaudet Apostle to the Deaf.* New York: St. Ann's Church for the Deaf, 1989.

Big River: The Adventures of Huckleberry Finn. Soundtrack. Decca U.S., 1988.

Bjorlee, Ignatius. "What Does Education Mean to You?" In *Sermons of the Deaf,* edited by J. M. Robertson, 19–23. Raleigh, NC: J. M. Robertson, 1954.

Braddock, Guilbert Campbell. "Ye Are Witnesses." *Silent Worker,* June 1952. Gallaudet University Archives. The Reverend Guilbert Campbell Braddock File.

Brodwin, Stanley. "Mark Twain in the Pulpit: The Theological Comedy of *Huckleberry Finn.*" In *One Hundred Years of* Huckleberry Finn: *The Boy, His Book, and American Culture,* edited by Robert Sattelmeyer and J. Donald Crowley, 371–85. Columbia: University of Missouri Press, 1985.

Brueggemann, Brenda Jo. *Lend Me Your Ears: Rhetorical Constructions of Deafness*. Washington, DC: Gallaudet University Press, 1999.

Buechner, Frederick. *Speak What We Feel (Not What We Ought to Say): Reflections on Literature and Faith*. San Francisco: HarperCollins, 2001.

Burch, Susan. "Biding the Time: American Deaf Cultural History, 1900 to World War II." PhD diss., Georgetown University, 1999.

———. "Capturing a Movement: Sign Language Preservation." *Sign Language Studies* 4, no. 3 (2004): 293–304.

———. *Signs of Resistance: American Deaf Cultural History*, 1900–1942. New York: New York University Press, 2002.

"The Burden of Deafness." *The Silent Worker* 31, no. 9 (June 1919): 166.

CAST. http://www.cast.org/.

"The Chapel." *Silent Worker* 12, no. 9 (May 1900): 136.

Christiansen, John B., and Sharon N. Barnartt. *Deaf President Now! The 1988 Revolution at Gallaudet University*. Washington, DC: Gallaudet University Press, 1995.

Cohen, Ron. "Big River: The Adventures of Huckleberry Finn." *Back Stage* 44, no. 32 (2003): 56.

Crouch, Barry A. and Brian H. Greenwald. "Hearing with the Eye: The Rise of Deaf Education in the United States." In *The Deaf History Reader*, edited by John Vickrey Van Cleve, 24–46. Washington, DC: Gallaudet University Press, 2007.

Daniell, Beth. *A Communion of Friendship: Literacy, Spiritual Practice, and Women in Recovery*. Carbondale: Southern Illinois University Press, 2003.

Daniels, Marilyn. *Benedictine Roots in the Development of Deaf Education: Listening with the Heart*. Westport, CT: Bergin and Garvey, 1997.

Deaf Missions. "Bible Visuals." http://www.deafmissions.com.

Deaf Opportunity OutReach (DOOR) International. http://www.doorinternational.com/.

"Deaf Worship, Socialize in Church of Their Own." *News Leader* (July 11, 1994). Gallaudet University Archives. Church Work with the Deaf File.

Fernandes, James John. *The Gate to Heaven: T. H. Gallaudet and the Rhetoric of the Deaf Education Movement*. PhD diss., University Michigan, 1980. UMI (8017260).

Fernandes, James J. and Jane F. Kelleher. "Signs of Eloquence: Selections from Deaf American Public Addresses." In *The Deaf Way: Perspectives from the International Conference on Deaf Culture*, edited by Carol J. Erting, et al,176–85. Washington, DC: Gallaudet University Press, 1994.

"Gallaudet to Honor Alumnus Who Carries Gospel to Deaf." *Washington Evening Star* 14 March 1930. Gallaudet University Archives. The Reverend Guilbert Campbell Braddock. File.

Gallaudet, Edward Miner. "The Combined System of Instruction." *American Annals of the Deaf* 36, no. 4 (October 1891): 255–65.

———. "The Ideal School for the Deaf." *American Annals of the Deaf* 37, no. 4 (October 1892): 280–85.

———. *History of the College for the Deaf, 1857–1907*. Washington, DC: Gallaudet College Press, 1983.

Gallaudet, Thomas Hopkins. "An Address Delivered at a Meeting for Prayer with Reference to the Sandwich Mission." *Early American Imprints*, 2nd ser (1819): fiche.

———. "Address to the Benevolent." *Connecticut Mirror* (1815): 14.

———. "A Sermon Delivered at the Opening of the Connecticut Asylum for the Education and Instruction of Deaf and Dumb Persons." *Early American Imprints*, 2nd ser., (1819): fiche.

Gannon, Jack R. *Deaf Heritage: A Narrative History of Deaf America*. Washington, DC: Gallaudet University Press, 2012.

———. *The Week the World Heard Gallaudet*. Washington, DC: Gallaudet University Press, 1989.

Garfield, Kim. "Deaf West Theatre: A Dream Come True." Center Theatre Group Performances: Mark Taper Forum. Playbill for *Big River: The Adventures of Huckleberry Finn* 1, no. 2 (December): 12–15.

"God Made Them All." *Arizona Cactus* 1, no. 2 (May 1926): 4.

Graybill, Patrick A. "Another New Birth: Reflections of a Deaf Native Signer." In *Cultural and Language Diversity and the Deaf Experience*, edited by Ila Parasnis, 225–31. New York: Cambridge University Press, 1996.

Greenwald, Brian H. "Taking Stock: Alexander Graham Bell and Eugenics, 1883-1922." In *Deaf History Reader*, edited by John Vickrey Van Cleve, 136–52. Washington, DC: Gallaudet University Press, 2007.

Griffin, Howard. "What Shall We Teach?" *Arizona Cactus* 1, no. 2 (May 1926): 6–7.

Hall, Percival. "The Truth about the Deaf, Their Sign Language, and Their Education." *Silent Worker* 26, no. 1 (October 1913): 15.

Hamilton, Leah. "The Desert." *Tucsonian* 2, no. 3 (June 1908): 30.

———. "The Lone Outlaw." *Tucsonian* 2, no. 3 (June 1908): 5.

Hasenstab, Philip J. "The Religious Training of the Deaf Child." *American Annals of the Deaf* 37, no. 1 (1892): 15–23.

Hauptman, William. *Big River: The Adventures of Huckleberry Finn, a Musical Play*. Adapted from the novel by Mark Twain. Music and lyrics by Roger Miller. New York: GrovePress, 1985.

Hays, John Q. "Mark Twain's Rebellion against God: Origins." *Southwestern American Literature* 3 (1973): 27–38.

Ho, Masami. "Heart Music in *Big River*." *Japan Times*, October 6, 2004, http://deafwest.org/productions/bigrivertourpress.html#japantimes.

Holland, Jeffrey R. "Soul-Butter and Hogwash: Mark Twain and Frontier Religion." In *"Soul-Butter and Hogwash" and Other Essays on the American West*, edited by Thomas G. Alexander, 5–32. Provo, UT: Brigham Young University Press, 1978.

Jankowski, Katherine A. *Deaf Empowerment: Emergence, Struggle, and Rhetoric*. Washington, DC: Gallaudet University Press, 1997.

Jenkins, W. G. "Professor A. Graham Bell's Studies on the Deaf." *Science* 16, no. 395 (August 29, 1890): 117–19.

"Just This Minute." *Arizona Cactus* 1, no. 1 (April 1926): 7.

Kannapell, Barbara. *Language Choice Reflects Identity Choice: A Sociolinguistic Study of Deaf College Students*. PhD diss. Georgetown University, 1985. Ann Arbor: UMI, 1986.

Knight, Hans. "Silent Sermon." *Philadelphia Inquirer*, August 29, 1965. Gallaudet University Archives. The Reverend Guilbert Campbell Braddock File.

Krentz, Christopher, ed. *A Mighty Change: An Anthology of Deaf American Writing, 1816–1864*. Washington, DC: Gallaudet University Press, 2000.

Lane, Harlan. *When the Mind Hears: A History of the Deaf*. New York: Vintage, 1984.

Leisman, Arthur G. "Prayers of the Deaf." In *Out of Silence*, edited by Arthur G. Leisman, 29. Milwaukee: Jackson Printing Co., 1947.

Long, J. Schuyler. *The Sign Language: A Man of Signs*, 2nd ed. Iowa City: Athens P, 1918.

Loring, George H. "George H. Loring's Address to Gallaudet." In *A Mighty Change: An Anthology of Deaf American Writing, 1816–1864*, edited by Christopher Krentz, 145–47. Washington, DC: Gallaudet University Press, 2000.

Manson, Alexander MacLeod. "The Work of the Protestant Churches for the Deaf in North America, 1815–1949." *American Annals of the Deaf* 95, no. 4 (1950): 387–433.

Martin, Joseph. "Lift Up Your Hands in the Sanctuary and Praise the Lord." *Bulletin* (March 1961). Gallaudet University Archives. St. Ann's Church File.

Mashburn, Arthur G. "The Sign-Language." *Silent Worker* 21, no. 5 (February 1909): 83.

Mattingly, Carol. *Well-Tempered Women: Nineteenth-Century Temperance Rhetoric*. Carbondale: Southern Illinois University Press, 2002.

Micotti, Alfred. "To the Sun." *Tucsonian* 3, no. 3 (December 1908): 9.

———. "Westward Ho." *Tucsonian* 3, no. 3 (December1908): 9.

Morgan, Gary and Judy Kegl. "Nicaraguan Sign Language and Theory of Mind: The Issue of Critical Periods and Abilities." *Journal of Child Psychology and Psychiatry* 47, no. 8 (August 2006): 811-19.

Mountford, Roxanne. *The Gendered Pulpit: Preaching in American Protestant Spaces*. Carbondale: Southern Illinois University Press, 2003.

National Association of the Deaf. http://www.nad.org.

"NAD Position Statement on Cochlear Implants." National Association of the Deaf. http://www.nad.org/issues/technology/assistive-listening/cochlear-implants.

Noll, Mark A. *A History of Christianity in the United States and Canada*. Grand Rapids, MI: Eerdmans, 1992.

———. *America's God: From Jonathan Edwards to Abraham Lincoln*. New York: Oxford University Press, 2002.

Padden, Carol A. "The People of the Eye." *Performances Magazine* 1, no. 2 (2002): 9–10.

———. "Translating Veditz." *Sign Language Studies* 4, no. 3 (2004): 244–59.

———, and Tom Humphries. *Deaf in America: Voices from a Culture*. Cambridge, MA: Harvard University Press, 1988.

———. 2005. *Inside Deaf Culture*. Cambridge, MA: Harvard University Press.

Pearson, Eliphalet. "Historic Sketch, Exhibited at the Opening of the Theological Institution." *Early American Imprints*, 2nd ser., (1801–1819):fiche.

Performing for Los Angeles Youth (PLAY). 2004. *Student Guide/Discovery Journal*. http://deafwest.org/productions/touring.html#educationcomponent.

———. 2004. *Teacher's Guide*. http://deafwest.org/productions/touring.html#educationcomponent.

Ramsey, Claire. *Deaf Children in Public Schools: Placement, Context, and Consequences*. Washington, DC: Gallaudet University Press, 1997.

"Religion and the Sign Language." *Silent Worker* 10, no. 10 (June 1898): 149.

Sasa Designs by the Deaf. "About." http://sasadesignsbythedeaf.com/sample-page/.

Sattelmeyer, Robert and J. Donald Crowley. *One Hundred Years of* Huckleberry Finn: *The Boy, His Book, and American Culture*. Columbia: University of Missouri Press, 1985.

Schirmer, Barbara R. *Psychological, Social, and Educational Dimensions to Deafness*. Boston: Allyn and Bacon, 2001.

Sexton, Clint C. "Religion for the Deaf." *Hoosier* 69, no. 7 (April 1957). Gallaudet University Archives. Church Work with the Deaf File.

Sound and Fury. Dir. Josh Aronson. Prod. Aronson Film Associates, 2000.

Spofford, Fisher Ames. "Fisher Ames Spofford's Address." In *A Mighty Change: An Anthology of Deaf American Writing, 1816–1864*, edited by Christopher Krentz, 142–45. Washington, DC: Gallaudet University Press, 2000.

St. Ann's Church Bulletin. (April 21, 1974). Gallaudet University Archives. St. Ann's Church File.

Stokoe, William C. *Language in Hand: Why Sign Came before Speech.* Washington, DC: Gallaudet University Press, 2001.

Strauss, Karen Peltz. *A New Civil Right: Telecommunications Equality for Deaf and Hard of Hearing Americans.* Washington, DC: Gallaudet University Press, 2006.

Vail, Thirza. "The Coming of Autumn." *Tucsonian* 3, no. 1 (December 1908): 12.

Valentine, Olivia. "The Deaf in History." *Arizona Cactus* 11, no. 5 (January 1936): 13.

Valentine, Phyllis. "Thomas Hopkins Gallaudet: Benevolent Paternalism and the Origins of the American Asylum." In *Deaf History Unveiled: Interpretations from the New Scholarship*, edited by John Vickrey Van Cleve, 53–73. Washington, DC: Gallaudet University Press, 1993.

Van Cleve, John V., and John Crouch. *A Place of Their Own: Creating the Deaf Community in America.* Washington, DC: Gallaudet University Press, 1989.

Veditz, George William. *Preservation of the Sign Language* [Film]. 1913. Gallaudet University Archives. George William Veditz (1861–1937) File.

Weeks, Stephen Beauregard. *History of Public Education in Arizona.* Department of the Interior Bureau of Education Bulletin, 1918, no. 17. Washington, DC.

Weld, Lewis. "The American Asylum." *American Annals of the Deaf* 1, no. 2 (January1948): 93–112.

"Why Do We Have a High School Paper?" *Tucsonian* 2, no. 3 (June 1908): 1–2.

Winefield, Richard. *Never the Twain Shall Meet: Bell, Gallaudet, and the Communications Debate.* Washington, DC: Gallaudet University Press, 1987.

Winship, F. M. 2003. "*Big River* Signed, Sung on Broadway." *United Press International* (August 5).

Woodward, James. *How You Gonna Get to Heaven If You Can't Talk with Jesus: On Depathologizing Deafness.* Silver Spring, MD: T.J. Publishers, 1982.

Index